Controller
Involvement
in Management

SATHE, Vijay. Controller involvement in management. Prentice-Hall, 1982. 189p bibl index 81-8515. 22.95 ISBN 0-13-171660-3. CIP
Sathe (Harvard) investigates the responsibilities of corporate controllers. Two questions are pursued: first, why controllers are more active in the decision-making process in some companies than in others and second, the consequences of controller involvement on company performance. Both questionnaire and personal interviews were conducted and the responses of over 400 executive officers of 24 large US corporations are tabulated and interpreted. The text is divided into three sections. Part I elaborates the importance of controller involvement in an organization. Part II develops and tests hypotheses concerning the business environment and controller involvement, concluding that the degree of controller involvement in a company's decision making is related to factors external to the controllers, that is, to characteristics of the company's environment, business, and management. Part III discusses the implications of the study for theory and practice, addressing such issues as recruitment, selection, placement, progression, continuing education, and the training of the corporate controller. The format is that of a doctoral dissertation with much discussion concerning the research methods used, and liberal quotation from the questionnaires and interviews. Exhibits, consisting of lists and charts, do little to enhance the understanding of the materials. An appendix reviews in detail the measurement techniques used. Excellent bibliography and index.

Controller
Involvement
in Management

VIJAY SATHE

Harvard University

With the research assistance of
Srinivasan Umapathy

Prentice-Hall, Inc., Englewood Cliffs, New Jersey 07632

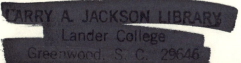

Library of Congress Cataloging in Publication Data

Sathe, Vijay.
   Controller involvement in management.

   Bibliography: p.
   Includes index.
   1. Controllership.   2. Industrial
management.   I. Title.
HG4026.S27   658.1'51   81-8515
ISBN 0-13-171660-3   AACR2

Editorial production supervision and interior design by *Barbara Grasso*
Cover design by *20/20*
Manufacturing buyer: *Edward O'Dougherty*

Printed in the United States of America

10   9   8   7   6   5   4   3   2   1

Prentice-Hall International, Inc., *London*
Prentice-Hall of Australia Pty. Limited, *Sydney*
Prentice-Hall of Canada, Ltd., *Toronto*
Prentice-Hall of India Private Limited, *New Delhi*
Prentice-Hall of Japan, Inc., *Tokyo*
Prentice-Hall of Southeast Asia Pte. Ltd., *Singapore*
Whitehall Books Limited, *Wellington, New Zealand*

Contents

Foreword   Herbert C. Knortz
            International Telephone & Telegraph Corporation   ix

Preface   xi

Acknowledgments   xiii

The Argument of the Book and the Findings in Brief   xv

PART I
A Dilemma for Controllers and Others   1

1   The Controller's Role in Management   6
     Definition of Controller Responsibilities   7
     Definition of Controller Involvement   9
     Importance of Controller Involvement   10
     Controller Influence Versus Involvement   16
     Controller Involvement Versus Independence   17

2   Controller Involvement and Company Performance   **21**

Controller Involvement and Financial Performance   *22*
Does Controller Involvement Stifle Management Creativity?   *23*
Controller Involvement Versus Independence   *25*
Patterns of Risk Taking, Control, Controller
     Involvement, and Performance   *27*
Case Appendix   *40*

PART II
Contextual Factors and Controller Involvement   **45**

3   Conceptual Framework and Research Methodology   **49**

Scope and Limitations   *49*
Conceptual Framework   *52*
Methodology   *54*

4   Degree of Corporate Controller Involvement at Headquarters   **64**

Contextual Factors and Controller Involvement   *64*
Reasons for Management's Varying Expectations
     Regarding Controller Involvement   *77*
Reasons for Management's Varying Expectations
     Regarding Controller Independence   *81*
Characteristics of the Corporate Controller   *83*

**5   Degree of Controller Involvement in a Division
of the Company**   **87**

Reexamination of Hypotheses in Chapter 4   *88*
Corporate Role in the Division   *91*
Reasons for Varying Degrees of Corporate Involvement
     in the Division   *92*

**6   Degree of Typical Division Controller Involvement in
the Company**   **98**

Environmental and Business Characteristics
     and Typical Division Controller Involvement   *99*
Corporate Management Characteristics and Typical
     Division Controller Involvement   *100*
Corporate Controller Characteristics and Typical
     Division Controller Involvement   *105*

PART III
Implications for Theory and Practice   113

7   Implictions for Research and Theory   115

Research on Controller Involvement   *115*
Implications for Descriptive Organization Theory   *117*
Implications for Prescriptive Organization Theory   *120*
Important Questions that Remain Unanswered   *125*

8   Implications for Practical Affairs   128

What Should the Role of the Division Controller Be?   *129*
Developing Strong Division Controllers   *140*
What Should the Role of the Corporate Controller Be?   *148*
What Should the Staff Role in Management Be?   *151*

Methodological Appendix   155

Bibliography   177

Index   183

Foreword

Controllership in the modern major corporation is an exciting and invigorating facet of managerial life—a facet that is vital to the success of corporate activities. Although the corporate community seems to respect and honor the control function, it tends to see controllership as a somewhat pedestrian and uncomplicated sphere of professionalism. It is appropriate, therefore, that an exploration be made of the most significant of the dichotomous tendencies that characterize this function.

In my opinion Vijay Sathe has correctly isolated the two principal poles—involvement and independence—around which controllership tends to gravitate. Wisely he has avoided an advocacy of either of the poles. He sees the involved controller as one who participates in and influences the process of decision making. On the other hand he sees the independent controller as one who provides an assurance of security and credibility to the basic financial process. In his conclusion he seems to assert that there is a need for both types, while stating that the emphasis on either aspect is dependent on environmental circumstances. These views appear to be consistent with operating experience.

The research method employed in investigating the dichotomous aspect of the controllership scene is of considerable interest. The use of statistical measurement techniques along with rather intensive and cross-validated interviewing procedures attests to the quantitative and qualitative verification of the findings. Obviously this technical carefulness adds to the general credibility and usefulness of the project. Although the author made a responsible effort to achieve a representative sample, it is somewhat unfortunate that the number of companies participating in the profile was limited to a mere two dozen.

It is quite obvious that the author has a firm understanding of the controller's world. He has perceived the nature of the conflicts around and within the corporate universe and has recognized the circumstances that permit the activist controller to increase his involvement in business decisions while permitting the more passive controller to render valuable service in monitoring the organization by the independence of his approach. The business universe that is presented in this book is a real world and the hypotheses that are presented for review are taken from daily experience. Both the academician and the practitioner are likely to feel comfortable with this portrayal of the American managerial scene.

Throughout this volume intriguing nuggets of organizational wisdom are presented to the readers. Three significant ones come immediately to mind. First, the author asserts that to a large degree a controller's job actually tends to become that type of performance that his superiors perceive that it should be. This suggests that an "involved" controller must convince his boss that involvement is essential. Second, it is stated that the "strong" controller can achieve an effective balance between independence and involvement. This suggests that the corporate and academic training of a controller should emphasize the development of a balanced executive rather than of an independence oriented professional. Third, it is noted that the strong controllers rely on the confrontation approach as their basic professional technique. This suggests that the means and boundaries of confrontation theory need greater consideration in the training process and in the behavior mode of practicing controllers.

The reading of this book should be a worthwhile experience to several different groups. The academician will enjoy it because it delineates the direction of changes in the training curriculum and hints at new areas of controllership research. The practicing executive will find it profitable because it points the way to the greater awareness and effectiveness of staff departments. The entrant to controllership practice will find useful the author's perception of the pulls and pressures, the circumstances and surroundings, and the arts and crafts that are the focus of this particular aspect of managerial life.

In general, the book represents a finely-tuned balance between the scholarly and the readable, between the useful and the entertaining, between the suggestive and the definitive. It is a fine piece of original investigation. I offer Vijay Sathe my professional congratulations and welcome his future probing of those myths, methods, and mysteries that in the past have played so prominent a role in my controllership career.

Herbert C. Knortz
Executive Vice President and Comptroller
International Telephone & Telegraph Corporation

Preface

This is a study of the controller's role in large business corporations. For the convenience of the busy reader, the argument of the book and the study findings are briefly summarized in a separate section immediately preceding the main text. Here I will only highlight one feature of this work that deserves special comment.

The book is addressed to both academicians and practitioners and deals with both theory and practice. This approach has its strengths and weaknesses. Among the strengths is the potential that both theory and practice may be enhanced. As the social psychologist Kurt Lewin pointed out many years ago, "There is nothing more practical than a good theory." Academicians can learn by trying to put their theories into practice.

One of the problems of this approach, however, is that practitioners and academicians represent very different audiences in terms of what they seek in a book, how they want material presented, and how much time they have to read it. Writing for these two diverse audiences in the same volume is a real challenge. My method has been to tailor each chapter to the audience likely to have the most interest in it and, as outlined in Part I, provide a "short cut" through the book for members of each audience.

A second difficulty faced by a study addressing these two audiences concerns the standards by which the work is judged. Academicians, even in professional fields such as business administration, tend to focus on questions of research methods and analytical rigor rather than questions of practical relevance and value. With practitioners the emphasis is reversed. They are more interested in ideas and suggestions that may help improve practice, even if these derive from "unscientific" data, such as a small sample size, or the opinions or behavior of particular managers in the study.

I have attempted to build on previous scholarly work by using the research methods and analytical techniques best suited to the task. However, where important practical questions could not be addressed with conventional research methods (e.g. in Chapter 2), I have addressed these problems as best I could rather than abandon the effort because a more rigorous approach was unavailable.

Despite the difficulties, I believe studies addressing both theoretical and practical concerns are needed in the interest of advancing theory and practice. This work is an attempt in that spirit.

Vijay Sathe
Associate Professor of Business Administration
Harvard University

Acknowledgments

Like others who have undertaken such a project, I find it difficult to properly acknowledge the contributions of all those who have helped me with it from inception to publication. However, I will attempt to recognize those who provided major assistance in rough chronological order.

Dr. J. Leslie Livingstone, my teacher, friend and erstwhile colleague, now with Coopers and Lybrand, sparked my initial interest in this subject area, and has continued to provide intellectual support, specific suggestions, and encouragement. Mr. Herbert C. Knortz of ITT has been a valuable source of assistance and ideas for many years. He not only provided extensive comments on the prepublication draft but has also written the foreword to this book. I owe much to these two men.

Nearly four hundred executives participated in this study. Without their generous support and time, the study would clearly not have been possible. My special thanks to these individuals and their companies, all of whom must necessarily remain anonymous.

As his place on the title page indicates, Professor Srinivasan Umapathy of Boston University made a significant contribution to this study as research assistant. Although he bears no responsibility for the basic conception and execution of this research, and was not involved in the writing of the book, his participation in field work and in computer analysis of the data were of enormous help.

The Associates of the Harvard Business School, through the Division of Research, provided generous financial support for the entire project. Professors Richard S. Rosenbloom and Stephen P. Bradley, Director and Associate Director, respectively, during the course of much of the project's life, gave steady assistance and encouragement, as did the present Director, Professor E. Raymond Corey.

A core group of five colleagues—Professors Robert N. Anthony, William J. Bruns, Jr., Paul R. Lawrence, Jay W. Lorsch, and Richard F. Vancil—comprised the intellectual sounding board for this study. They offered guidance throughout the course of the project and provided critical comments and suggestions on numerous occasions. If there are strengths in this book, much of the credit goes to these five individuals.

I have benefited from the help of other colleagues at Harvard who discussed and critiqued this work at various stages, particularly Professors Chris Argyris and John Dearden. Professor Richard E. Walton's insightful criticism at a critical juncture saved me much grief later on as did the valuable comments and suggestions received from Professor Edward E. Lawler III of the University of Southern California.

Professor William W. Cooper, now at the University of Texas, and Professors Robert G. Eccles, Tamar Frankel, Thomas B. Lifson, Kenneth D. Merchant, and Henry B. Reiling of Harvard graciously read the working draft of this book and provided helpful comments. So did several controllers and other managers in the participating companies who, for reasons of confidentiality, must regretfully remain anonymous. These detailed critiques were of great help in preparing the final draft.

Professor John P. Kotter was always a source of ideas and strength. Without his help in managing my other responsibilities at Harvard, I would not have been able to devote the necessary energy and attention to this study.

Ms. Catherine Hunt, whom I am most fortunate to have as a secretary, typed all the exhibits, read drafts of the manuscript (always defending the reader's right to clarity), and provided the kind of first-rate assistance that permits a professor to write a book.

Ms. Rose Giacobbe, Supervisor of the Word Processing Center at Harvard Business School, and her associates, Millie Metro, Vera Pawlowskis, Barbard Regan, Pat Rivera, and Aimee Hamel, produced minor miracles by keeping the typing on schedule (even though I did not always hand them the material on time!). My special thanks to them.

Prentice-Hall editor Theodore K. Jursek was very supportive of this book from the outset and always came through with the needed assistance.

Finally, I owe a special debt of gratitude to my wife Shanu for her faith, encouragement, and support throughout the course of this venture, and to our four-year-old Sheila, who never really understood what daddy was up to in his study but let him be nonetheless.

While I wish to acknowledge all these debts, I gladly accept full responsibility for the final product. The project produced much personal learning and was fun. I hope the reader finds some of both in the following pages.

Vijay Sathe
Associate Professor of Business Administration
Harvard University

The Argument of the Book and the Findings in Brief

In an economy plagued by business recessions, inflation, capital shortages, and general economic uncertainty, managers are well aware of the importance of the controller's role. How the role may be better performed is less well understood, however. It is the subject of this book.

Because the research was conducted within a conceptual framework based on recent developments in organization theory, the findings and their implications should be of interest not only to practitioners—both controllers and other managers—but also to academicians, particularly those in the organizational behavior and behavioral accounting areas. About four hundred managers in twenty-four large U.S. corporations in ten basic industries completed questionnaires and were interviewed for this book.

Unlike operating executives, controllers are staff managers and not measured on operating profit and loss (the "bottom line"). How should their performance be assessed? According to conventional thinking an appropriate criterion of effectiveness is the quality of information and analysis presented to aid operating executives in business decision making. I argue that this is too simplistic a view in today's business environment. Because of increasing organizational size and business complexity the operating executives, however bright and capable, simply do not have the depth of knowledge in the variety of disciplines needed to achieve maximum effectiveness. Making quality information and analysis available is no assurance that it will be brought to bear when decisions are made. Staff executives such as the controller must become actively involved in the business decision-making process— by recommending courses of action and by challenging the plans and actions of operating executives—to ensure that specialist knowledge and expertise get proper consideration when business decisions and actions are taken.

What can be done to enhance such involvement? Although the controller's personality, motivation, and skill are an important part of the answer, the question is first addressed from the standpoint of senior corporate management seeking to increase the general level of controller involvement in the company. To do so, concepts from the field of organizational behavior (role theory and contingency theory of organization) are drawn upon. These indicate that context influences behavior. In Part II of the book, specific hypotheses are generated and examined with data, and descriptive "models" are developed to understand the extent to which various contextual factors, that is, environmental, business, and management variables, influence the level of controller involvement in business decision making.

This part of the book will be of particular interest to academicians because it shows the power and limits of modern organization theory in explaining behavior in a particular setting, that is, involvement of the controller. Although these data and analyses generally support the "situational perspective" now well established in theories of organizational behavior—because they indicate that controller involvement is systematically related to the context in which the controller operates—they also suggest that current theory and research tends to underestimate the important influence of management's expectations, orientation, operating style, and management philosophy.

Since the models of controller involvement relate various contextual factors to controller involvement, situational "levers" available to produce change are suggested. Depending on the manager's vantage point in the organization, one or more of these levers may be used to alter the constraints and opportunities for controller involvement, that is, the "context" for involvement. Whatever the particular context, however, it is possible to increase the level of involvement on the bases of individual motivation, personal initiative, and the acquisition of certain skills described in the book.

In addition to the controller's role of contribution in business decisions, calling for active involvement in management, the controller is responsible for the accuracy of financial reporting and for the integrity of internal control. These latter two responsibilities are also growing in importance because of the public disclosures concerning corporate illegal payments, and the perception that corporate bribery has been concealed by falsification of corporate books and records. For example, the Foreign Corrupt Practices Act enacted by the U.S. Congress in 1977 is not limited to foreign transactions. It requires that companies under the jurisdiction of the Securities and Exchange Commission must adhere to strict accounting and internal control standards. Both companies and their executives are subject to civil and criminal liability if they do not comply.

Because of these developments, most corporations today have strengthened their internal audit staff. However, even if the corporation has a strong internal audit staff, who periodically visit the field locations, this group cannot offer the *continuous* vigilance that the local controller can. Neither do internal auditors typically have the depth of knowledge about local systems, people, and practices to be able to detect subtle misrepresentations or inadequacies. Thus, the corporation must rely on the local controller to be an effective local guardian. Is such a role—that of "policeman" or "umpire in a ball game"—inconsistent with the role of active participant in the business decision-making process? Can the controller wear these two hats effectively—one requiring a degree of involvement, the other a degree of independence?

I argue that the answer is—it depends. Many controllers and operating executives *believe* that controller involvement and controller independence are more or less mutually exclusive. Emphasis on one makes effective performance of the other more difficult. However, "strong" controllers are able to overcome this apparent dilemma and remain actively involved while retaining independence. The key lies in the development of certain personal qualities and interpersonal and other skills described in the book.

Strong controllers constitute a vital corporate strength not only because contribution in two areas is better than contribution in one, but more importantly because *before*-the-fact or anticipatory control results. A controller actively involved in business decisions has access to all sensitive information and deliberations in progress. Such a controller has an opportunity to put a stop to ill-conceived, ill-advised, or illegal decisions and actions *before* they are taken. A controller not actively involved is not privy to such information and can only provide after-the-fact or reactive control.

While acknowledging the importance of more responsive, before-the-fact control, some would argue that the way to accomplish this is by holding *general managers* accountable, not by relying on the controllers. Although general managers at each organizational level are of course fully accountable to general management at higher levels for these and other areas of responsibility, higher level general management may seek a system of checks and balances in areas of particular concern to them. The underlying motivation may not be fully appreciated by those unfamiliar with the contemporary legal environment. Personal liability today is generally seen to be an exanding concept—managers are liable not only for known actions and decisions as in the past, but increasingly for those they *should have* known about. This expanded interpretation of culpability increases the importance of securing valid information from managers at lower levels—preferably *before* decisions and actions in particularly sensitive areas are taken. Hence the understandable desire for a system of checks and balances.

Despite these benefits of operating with strong controllers, they are not a panacea. The costs of this approach must be weighed against the potential benefits and compared with those for alternatives open to management. One option is to emphasize controller involvement or controller independence, but not both. Another is to split the controller's role—assigning the responsibility for involvement to one individual and for independence to another. These alternatives demand less of the controller in terms of personal qualities and interpersonal and other skills, but have their own disadvantages. Management needs to determine what type of role for the controller is best suited to its own particular situation. I provide guidelines to make this assessment.

One logical extension of this analysis yields guidelines for use by the board of directors in determining what the role of the corporate controller should be. If different from the role of the corporate controller as currently performed, the board may wish to recommend a change in the needed direction. Although they may be difficult to implement for a number of reasons, such recommendations *logically* follow from my data and analysis. They are meant to provoke a discussion of whether current practice in this area, whether derived from company law or corporate tradition, is really in the best interest of the common stockholder.

Another extension of the analysis based on logical analogy provides guidelines with direct relevance for other staff roles, for example, personnel and legal, now increasingly experiencing the dual pressures of the controller's role. On the one hand, increasing organizational size and complexity call for greater involvement from those in these positions to ensure that specialist expertise and judgment are brought to bear when business decisions are made. On the other hand, mounting external pressures from litigation and regulation require persons in these positions to retain a sense of objectivity and independence from affiliated management.

The apparent contradiction in the requirements for staff involvement *and* staff independence has not been adequately addressed in either theory or practice. A conceptual scheme for examining this question is proposed. Guidelines for practitioners interested in the development of strong staff—those able to remain actively involved while retaining independence—are also suggested.

part I

A Dilemma for Controllers and Others

Like some other roles in management, the controller has two seemingly contradictory responsibilities, both of which appear to be increasing in importance.

On the one hand, the controller is responsible for providing assistance in the business decision-making process. Conditions today are such that managers are well aware of the importance of this aspect of the controller's role. In an economy plagued by business recessions, inflation, capital shortages, and general economic uncertainty, managers have come to depend more than ever on sound financial analysis and control. Business recessions have sharply emphasized the critical need for effective cost control and asset management. And continuing inflation and capital shortages have made managers keenly aware of the importance of achieving high returns on stockholders' equity, requiring sound financial management and capital investment. Also, the growing complexity of business combined with the general economic uncertainty has led to the increased use of planning and other analytical techniques requiring good financial information. The controller can make important contributions in these areas by becoming actively involved in the business decision-making process.

On the other hand, the controller is also responsible for the integrity of the financial information provided to external agencies and for ensuring that control practices conform to corporate policy and procedures. To discharge these responsibilities effectively, the controller must retain a sense of objectivity and independence from management. The recent public disclosures concerning kickbacks and illegal payments have made corporations extremely sensitive to the need for strict controls throughout the organization and have served to highlight the importance of controller independence. For example, the Foreign Corrupt Practices Act enacted by the U.S. Congress in 1977 is not limited to matters either foreign or corrupt.

1

It covers all transactions, and to comply with the provisions of the law an adequate system of internal controls must be maintained. Both companies and their executives are subject to civil and criminal liability for noncompliance. Other external pressures are the growing number of auditing rules and reporting requirements with which the corporation must comply. Recent examples include rules covering replacement cost accounting and reporting of profit and loss resulting from currency fluctuations. These and other demands for information from stockholders, the government, and regulatory agencies emphasize the growing importance of controller independence.

As the title suggests, this book is focused on the controller's involvement in the business decision-making process. However, the consequences of such involvement for controller independence are also considered. It is based on a field investigation of two dozen large, industrial corporations (annual revenues in excess of $300 million). In these companies, there is a controller at corporate headquarters—the corporate controller—as well as controllers at other organizational levels. This study is concerned primarily with the degree of involvement of the company's controllers collectively and less so with the degree of involvement of a controller in a particular location, that is, with the basic unit of analysis as the company, rather than a division of a company or an individual controller in a division. However, involvement of controllers in particular locations within the company is also considered.

Two broad questions are pursued. First, why is it that in some companies controllers are involved more actively in the business decision-making process than in others? Although there may be variations in controller involvement within the same company, and these are examined, why is it that in some companies the general level of involvement is greater than in others? To the extent that factors affecting the degree of controller involvement can be identified, and their influence understood, it becomes possible to think in terms of avenues available for making needed changes. Management seeking to increase the general level of controller involvement in the company could ask this question: "What 'levers' do we have available to produce change?"

The second question concerns the consequences of controller involvement for company performance. Does active controller involvement help improve the company's financial performance? Does active controller involvement compromise controller independence? Does involvement stifle management creativity and initiative? These are important practical questions, but they are extremely difficult to investigate because a multitude of factors affects a company's performance. How does the researcher isolate the controller's contribution as a result of involvement in business decisions? The approach taken here is to compare companies with greater and lesser degrees of controller involvement to gain some understanding of the related consequences for the company.

This book has relevance beyond the controller's role. There are other staff positions in which the responsibilities for assisting and monitoring the activities of affiliated management are *both* increasing in importance. On the one hand, because of increasing organizational size and complexity, management relies more than ever on specialist advice and expertise. Active staff involvement increases the likelihood that the appropriate specialized knowledge and judgment will be brought to bear when business decisions are made. On the other hand, as the modern corporation experiences mounting external pressures from litigation and regulation, the importance of staff independence for positions such as personnel and quality assurance is also increasing. For instance, increased exposure to product liability claims is making the maintenance of appropriate quality standards more critical; government regulations concerning equal employment opportunity and occupational safety and health are making compliance in these areas more vital than ever. Since controllers have had the dual responsibility for both assisting and monitoring the activities of affiliated management for a long time, what is learned by examining the controller's role has direct relevance for other staff positions now increasingly facing the same situation.

Data collection for this research involved a day of interviews at corporate head-quarters and a day in two or three business units of each of the 24 corporations studied. A profile of these companies is included in Exhibit I-1. Fourteen executives were interviewed at each company, including the chief executive officer, the corporate controller, and other corporate executives as well as general managers and controllers in the business units. Interviews were typically one hour long. Questionnaires were also mailed to the participants in advance of the interviews to facilitate data collection. Thus, the results reported in this book are both qualitative, that is, observations and comments from the interviews, and quantitative, that is, statistical analysis of questionnaire and interview responses.

The book is organized into three parts. Part I begins with a more complete elaboration of the importance of controller involvement and why the subject has increasing relevance for other staff positions (Chapter 1); it concludes with data and discussion on the consequences of controller involvement for company financial performance, for controller independence, and for management creativity and initiative (Chapter 2). The analysis and tone of discussion in this first part of the book are qualitative rather than quantitative. Observations and quotations rather than statistical correlations are used to support the argument made.

In Part II hypotheses are generated and descriptive models of how various factors influence the degree of controller involvement are developed. Following a detailed discussion of the conceptual framework and methodology used to direct this research (Chapter 3), an analysis of how various factors are related to the degree of corporate controller involvement at headquarters is presented (Chapter 4). This analysis is then used to study the analogous phenomenon within a division of the company (Chapter 5) and leads to a "top-down" perspective on the degree of typical division controller involvement in the company (Chapter 6). In contrast to the first part of the book, the analysis and tone of discussion in the second part are more quantitative and formal. Hypotheses are developed, the underlying rationale is discussed, and the statistical results are presented. Quotations from the interview notes are sometimes used to illustrate the findings.

Exhibit I-1   Profile of the Companies Studied

Profile	Number of Companies
Revenues	
$300-499 million	7
$500-999 million	4
$1-3 billion	8
Over $5 billion	5
	24
Industry category	
Chemicals	2
Conglomerates	4
Construction and building equipment	4
Energy	3
Foods	4
Forest products and packaging	2
Health care products	1
Industrial equipment	1
Information processing	2
Metals	1
	24
Financial performance relative to industry average[a]	
Considerably above average	6
Above average	5
Average	4
Below average	5
Considerably below average	4
	24

[a]See variable D1 in the Methodological Appendix for an explanation of how financial performance was measured.

Part III is a discussion of the implications of this study for theory (Chapter 7) and practice (Chapter 8). The Methodological Appendix at the end of the book contains information on the specific questions asked in the interviews and in the questionnaires, along with a description of how the responses were combined to obtain various measurements.

Because this book is written for both practitioners and academicians, the reader may wish to pick and choose topics of the greatest interest. Judging from the comments received from those who read earlier drafts of this book, managers are more interested in useful ideas and practical insights and less in details concerning methodology or data analysis. With researchers and theorists the emphasis is reversed. Accordingly, the following "shortcuts" through the book are provided in an attempt to make the findings of this study more accessible to members of both audiences.

Shortcut for Managers: Chapters 1, 2, 4 (perhaps), and 8

Chapter 1 is an elaboration of why the subject of controller involvement is important and how it has relevance for other staff roles in management. In Chapter 2 the discussion of how controller involvement is related to company performance is more fully developed. Questions about whether increased controller involvement improves company financial performance, whether involvement compromises controller independence, and whether it stifles management creativity and initiative are all addressed here using qualitative data and comparative analysis. Descriptive models of how various contextual factors influence controller involvement are developed in Part II and are summarized in Exhibits 4-7 and 6-4. If the reader is interested in getting some flavor for the rationale underlying these models, Chapter 4 provides a good illustration of how these models were developed. Chapter 8 is a detailed discussion of the implications of this study for practical affairs.

Shortcut for Researchers and Theorists: Chapters 1, 3, 4, 5, 6, and 7

Chapter 1 provides a general orientation to the subject matter of the research. Details concerning the conceptual framework and the methodology are in Chapter 3. (The specific questionnaire, interview schedules, and procedures used in the measuring variables are included in the Methodological Appendix.) The hypotheses relating various contextual factors to controller involvement are generated in the next three chapters and are the basis for the development of descriptive models—of the corporate controller's involvement at headquarters (Chapter 4), of a controller in a division of the company (Chapter 5), and of the typical controller involvement in the company (Chapter 6). Implications of this study for research and theory are considered in Chapter 7.

While providing these shortcuts through the book, it is hoped that readers will be sufficiently intrigued with the subject matter to read the entire book.

chapter 1

The Controller's Role in Management

The position of controller in American business appears to have been first created in the 1880s when several railroad companies established the office of "comptroller."[1] During these early years the controller handled routine accounting matters, preparation of financial records, and custody of the company's assets. Gradually the controller's role broadened to include the analysis and explanation of financial facts and figures in order to assist management in the running of the business. As one book on controllership put it:

> the controller is not the commander of the ship—that is the task of the chief executive—but he may be likened to the navigator, the one who keeps the charts. He must keep the commander informed as to how far he has come, where he is, what speed he is making, resistance encountered, variations from the course, dangerous reefs which lie ahead, and where the charts indicate he should go next in order to reach the port in safety.[2]

[1] The word "comptroller" came into use because of an error in translation from the Latin original. The more correct spelling, "controller," is now commonly used in industry. However, the "erroneous" method of spelling continues to be used in some businesses because of tradition and in most public agencies because it is part of the official scribes, for example, Comptroller of the Currency and Comptroller General of the United States.

[2] Heckert and Willson (1952), p. 4. (All references refer to the alphabetically ordered bibliography at the end of the book. The year of publication is in parentheses.)

essential

This broadening of the controller's role was further emphasized with the formation of the Controllers Institute of America in 1931, an organization dedicated to enhancing the professional standards of controllership. In 1962 the institute formally recognized the greatly expanded responsibility of its membership and changed its name to the Financial Executives Institute.

DEFINITION OF CONTROLLER RESPONSIBILITIES

According to the Financial Executives Institute, financial management responsibilities may be divided into two major functions—controllership and treaureship.[3] A list of the specific areas of responsibility assigned to each of these functions is shown in Exhibit 1-1. This study is concerned with the controllership responsibilities only.

Exhibit 1-1   Controllership and Treasurership Functions Defined by Financial Executives Institute[a]

The Function of Treasurership	The Function of Controllership
1. Provision of capital. To establish and execute programs for the provision of the capital required by the business, including negotiating the procurement of capital and maintaining the required financial arrangements.	1. Planning for control. To establish, coordinate, and administer, as an integral part of management, an adequate plan for the control of operations. Such a plan would provide, to the extent required in the business, profit planning, programs for capital investing and for financing, sales forecasts, expense budgets, and cost standards, together with the necessary procedures to effectuate the plan.
2. Investor relations. To establish and maintain an adequate market for the company's securities and, in connection therewith, to maintain adequate liaison with investment bankers, financial analysts, and shareholders.	2. Reporting and interpreting. To compare performance with operating plans and standards and to report and interpret the results of operations to all levels of management and to the owners of the business. This function includes the formulation of accounting policy, the coordination of systems and procedures, and the preparation of operating data and of special reports as required.
3. Short-term financing. To maintain adequate sources for the company's current borrowings from commercial banks and other lending institutions.	3. Evaluating and consulting. To consult with all segments of management responsible for policy or action concerning any phase of the operation of the business as it relates
4. Banking and custody. To maintain banking arrangements; to receive, have custody of, and disburse the company's monies and securities; and to be responsible for the financial aspects of real estate transactions.	
5. Credits and collections. To direct the granting of credit and the	

[3] Harkins (1969), p. 19.

Exhibit 1-1 (continued)

The Function of Treasurership	The Function of Controllership
collection of accounts due the company, including the supervision of required special arrangements for financing sales, such as time payment and leasing plans.	to the attainment of objectives and the effectiveness of policies, organization structure, and procedures.
6. Investments. To invest the company's funds as required and to establish and coordinate policies for investment in pension and other similar trusts.	4. Tax administration. To establish and administer tax policies and procedures.
	5. Government reporting. To supervise or coordinate the preparation of reports to government agencies.
7. Insurance. To provide insurance coverage as required.	6. Protection of assets. To ensure protection for the assets of the business through internal control and internal auditing and by ensuring proper insurance coverage.
	7. Economic appraisal. To appraise economic and social forces and government influences continuously and to interpret their effect upon the business.

[a]Reported in Harkins (1969), p. 19.

Source: Edward P. Harkins, "Organizing and Managing the Corporate Financial Function," Business Policy Study No. 129 (New York: National Industrial Conference Board, 1969), p. 19.

From Exhibit 1-1, the controller's areas of responsibility may be summarized as follows:

1. preparation of reports for stockholders and government agencies (responsibilities 4 and 5)
2. protection of assets (6)
3. provision of information and analysis to assist management in the running of the business (1, 2, 3, and 7)

This study is focused on the third area of responsibility, specifically the degree of controller involvement in business decision making. However, implications for the other two areas of responsibility are also explored. The term "controller" in this study refers to the person primarily responsible for the controllership function. Since other executives may be engaged in controllership responsibilities to varying degrees,[4] this factor is considered along with many others in explaining the degree of controller involvement in business decision making.

[4] There are historical, political, personal, and other reasons for this. In a study of 25 controllers in small- and medium-sized companies, Moseley (1972) found that persons with a variety of titles other than "controller" were engaged in controller-

The corporations included in this study are large industrial firms with revenues exceeding $300 million. These companies have controllers at several organizational levels. All have a controller at corporate headquarters—the corporate controller—as well as a controller in each of the company's business units or divisions—division controllers. Depending on the corporate organization and management philosophy, there may also be a group controller for each grouping of business units. In addition, there may be plant controllers in manufacturing plants and controllers in the marketing or purchasing departments. In this book the focus is on the corporate and division controller positions only. Further, the primary focus is on the degree of involvement of the company's controllers collectively and less so on the degree of involvement of a controller in a particular position within the company.

DEFINITION OF CONTROLLER INVOLVEMENT

In the typical large, multidivisional corporation, the controller positions studied are almost always considered to be a part of "the management team." Thus, the question of controller involvement is not whether or not these controllers partake in the business decision-making process. They invariably do. However, the *degree* to which they participate in decision making varies.

Consider the variety of activities in which the controller is involved with management in the modern industrial enterprise. An important set of management tasks in these organizations concerns the annual planning and budgeting process. While the form, timing, and attention devoted to these activities vary from company to company, the controller is typically involved in the numerous business evaluations that must be made. Another important set of controller interactions with management occurs in connection with the periodic review of financial performance. In today's large corporations, these reviews take place every month, with a more comprehensive and detailed accounting of performance quarterly. In many companies executives from the headquarters and field locations meet face to face to discuss these periodic results, especially at the quarterly reviews. In the field locations, local controllers are typically involved in the periodic review of operating performance conducted by the general managers. In most cases, managers and controllers meet and discuss results before sending them up to corporate headquarters and also "dry run" or "rehearse" budget and planning presentations prior to the actual session with corporate executives.

Beyond these activities that take place on a programmed basis, a multitude of controller-manager interactions occur on a nonprogrammed basis with varying degrees of intensity and frequency. These involve questions about advertising, promotion, distribution, credit, inventory, or pricing to name just a few. The controller may be involved in special studies on new facilities, new products, and other invest-

---

ship responsibilities, for example, treasurer, director of profit planning, auditor, vice president of finance. Sometimes, no executive had the title of "controller." In the present study, the person primarily engaged in controllership responsibilities most often had the formal title of "controller."

ments including acquisitions. In the case of multidivisional companies, controllers are frequently involved in pricing of intracompany transfers of goods and services and other interdivisional matters.

Given the range of activities in which the controller may be involved with management in business decision making, how does one identify the degree of controller involvement? Beyond qualitative information obtained via interviews with controllers and other managers, an attempt was made to quantify the degree of controller involvement via a questionnaire that asked managers to indicate the intensity with which controllers were expected to perform various roles as participants in operating and strategic business decisions and the degree to which they actually did so, that is, role of presenting information and analysis, recommending action, and challenging plans and actions of operating executives.

The notion of active controller involvement in this study thus encompasses not only the presentation of information and analysis to aid management in business decision making but also the recommending of courses of action to be taken and the challenging of plans and actions of operating executives. Examples are recommendations and challenges with regard to questions such as the following: Is the sales forecast too optimistic? Are the receivables and inventory levels optimal? Is the promotion and advertising budget appropriate? Are the financial estimates in the capital investment plan and the new product development proposal realistic? It is one thing to be able to make recommendations and challenge management in the areas of accounting policy or internal control where defined rules and procedures exist. It is quite another thing to be able to recommend and question business decisions and actions in areas where clear guidelines or answers do not exist.

IMPORTANCE OF CONTROLLER INVOLVEMENT

There are three major reasons why a study of controller involvement is both interesting and important. First, the phenomenon has been of interest to practitioners for a very long time. Much of the trade and practitioner literature suggests that controller involvement is on the rise, but this has never been systematically determined. Second, the limited number of prior studies on controller involvement suggests that controllers are not as actively involved in the decision-making process as either they or their managers would like. However, the *reasons* for this have not been sufficiently explored. Finally, the literature on line and staff positions indicates that those in staff roles, that is, controllers, personnel managers, quality control managers, need to be actively involved in business decision making to be effective. These three bodies of literature are now reviewed.

Trade and Practitioner Literature

According to reports in trade journals, articles in the business press, and practitioner-oriented books and publications, the controller's involvement in management has been increasing for some time. *Business Week,* for example, dramatized this trend in a cover story devoted to the rise of the controller and attributed it mainly to the increased importance of financial analysis and control in the wake of the business recession of 1973-1974 and double-digit inflation:

> Only 10 years ago, most controllers were relegated to obscurity, to adding the debits and credits and reporting what had already happened. . . . Controllers are now getting involved with the operating side of the company, where they give advice and influence production, marketing, and investment decisions as well as corporate planning.[5]

A *Harvard Business Review* article indicates that with internal cash generation growing in importance the financial executive's involvement in operating decisions is much greater today than it was in the late 1960s. As a result, the authors maintain, the borders between finance and operations have blurred noticeably in recent years.[6]

In the late 1960s, when the financial executives's involvement was presumably less than it is today, a report from the National Industrial Conference Board stated that

> The corporate controller has emerged over the past few years from relative obscurity to a position of considerable importance and influence. The emphasis of his job has changed from collecting and recording data to making better information available for running and controlling the business.[7]

Similar observations were made in a report that appeared at about the same time in *Dun's Review:*

> The controller, the man whose job it used to be to keep the books and say "no," is now a key executive who is showing management what it *can* do—and how to do it . . . not only is he ferreting out the trouble spots, he is suggesting ways of fixing them. And it is this role of decision maker that has elevated him to the highest circles of management.[8]

This article linked the rise of the controller to both the advent of the computer, which presumably allowed a refocusing of effort from the production of numbers to their analysis and use in decision making, as well as to the increasing numbers of business graduates, including MBAs, trained in the use of analytical techniques and seeking careers in controllership.

The relatively passive role that the controller supposedly played in the past is not evident in reports published in the 1950s, or even in the 1940s, however.[9]

[5] "The Controller: Inflation Gives Him More Clout with Management," *Business Week*, August 15, 1977, p. 84.

[6] Gerstner and Anderson (1976).

[7] Harkins (1969), p. 32.

[8] Poindexter (1969), pp. 37, 39.

[9] Bradshaw and Hull (1950); Bradshaw (1950); Jackson (1949).

Apparently, each generation of writers on this subject has perceived the controller's role to be on the rise. Whether in fact this reported trend is an accurate portrayal of the history of the controller's involvement in management is unclear. The opinions offered are typically based on personal experience and observation. Further, a large bulk of this literature is written by controllers themselves.

If national compensation practices are examined, one finds that the percentage increase in average annual compensation for controllers has not been greater than has that for other senior executives during the 1970s.[10] To the extent that such data on relative pay scales reflect relative importance of various positions, the importance of the controller's role does not appear to have increased *relative to* those of other managers—at least since 1970, the period for which data are available.

Studies of Controller Involvement

There have been few systematic studies of controller involvement in decision making. One is the study of controllership in department stores published by Helfert and his colleagues.[11] This study found that the controller was frequently unable to realize the full potential of that role and did not exert significant influence over operating decisions. Both formal aspects of the controller's role, such as title and status (typically one or two levels removed from the chief executive), and other factors (such as negative attitudes of the controller or management) were identified as possible reasons.

Another is a recent study by Hopper[12] of 12 management accountants in six companies in the United Kingdom. The study found that, although a majority of the accountants *and* the managers with whom they worked desired greater decision-making involvement for the accountants, this was not in fact happening. A major reason for this was that the bookkeeping activities, which were clearly defined and programmed to a rigid schedule, took up considerable time and attention. In contrast, the liaison and service activities, which offered the opportunity for greater involvement in the business decision-making process, lacked formal specification and were consequently neglected. This phenomenon of the "hard" driving out the "soft" was also reported in an earlier study by Simon and his colleagues,[13] who recommended a separation of the bookkeeping and service functions to overcome the difficulty.

The research findings on the controller's involvement in decision making are thus similar—controllers are less actively involved in the process than both they and other managers would like. (The same finding was reported in a study of another staff position—that of the personnel manager.)[14]

[10] Mruk and Giardina (1977).

[11] Helfert, May, and McNair (1965), particularly pp. 91-109.

[12] Hopper (1978).

[13] Simon, Guetzkow, Kozmetsky, and Tyndall (1954).

[14] Belasco and Alutto (1969).

Additional reasons for this involvement "gap" not mentioned in these studies could be cited. First is the rather colorless image of the controller in the minds of some managers. One study found that, while it appears to be inappropriate and unwarranted, the accountant is stereotyped as cold, aloof, and impersonal.[15] Although a study of accountants in public accounting firms, rather than in industrial organizations, it is relevant because many controllers begin their careers as public accountants. Other unflattering images of the controller are well known to practitioners, that is, "bean counter," "number cruncher," "green eyeshade." This stereotyping could affect the quality of the controller's relationships with management and consequently the degree of controller involvement.

It is also possible that some controllers do in fact develop a conservative attitude because of their background in public accounting and because of their stewardship responsibilities.[16] A related factor that may influence interpersonal relationships with management, and hence controller involvement, is the fact that controllers provide information that is used to evaluate management performance.[17] In reporting operating results, explaining causes of variance, and commenting on the actions taken by operating managers, the controller can become the bearer of bad news. Unless this unhappy duty is performed with sensitivity and skill, the controller's working relationships with management could be impaired and involvement in decision making adversely affected.[18]

The research evidence cited does not necessarily refute the trade and business press reports that suggest increasing controller involvement over the years. It does indicate that controller involvement in decision making falls short of both the controllers' own expectations and those of the managers with whom they work. Thus, even if the controllers' involvement in management has been on the rise as the trade and business press suggests, the research evidence indicates that there is room for greater involvement.

Literature on Line and Staff

The terms "line" and "staff" probably originated in military organizations. The use of staff in armies dates back to at least 1500 B.C. when Thothmes set up a form of intelligence service and an administrative system for his command in Egypt.[19] Widespread use of staff in American business followed the Great Depression of the 1930s when the importance of planning and control, complexities of labor relations, expansion of government regulation, and proliferation of legal and accounting problems arising from new legislation all made increased staff assistance necessary.[20]

[15] DeCoster and Rhode (1971).
[16] Lawler and Rhode (1976).
[17] Harrell (1961).
[18] Hassler and Harlan (1958), p. 5.
[19] Lawler and Rhode (1976), p. 112.
[20] Koontz and O'Donnell (1976), p. 340.

The distinction between line and staff as traditionally applied to business organizations is based on a division of organizational work into "operational work" and "specialist work."[21] Operational work consists of the basic tasks of any business—development, production, and sale of a product or service. These jobs are considered to be within the direct chain of command—the line—from which persons in these positions derive their formal authority. Specialist work consists of tasks performed in support of operational work, for example, accounting, law, personnel, public relations, purchasing, research. These jobs—the staff—fall outside the direct chain of command, and persons in these positions lack direct formal authority over persons in line positions.

Although the distinction between line and staff is one of the oldest in literature on organization, according to one popular management text there is "probably no area of management which in practice causes more difficulties, more friction, and more loss of time and effectiveness."[22] Much of the line-staff conflict stems from the fact that the staff must work through the line to get their ideas and suggestions implemented. The differences in backgrounds and orientations between those in line and staff positions also contribute to the problem.[23] As organizations have grown larger and more complex, the number of staff positions has increased to cope with the increased demand for specialist knowledge and expertise, thus intensifying the difficulties.[24]

To ease these difficulties, several writers on organization have suggested that the staff be given formal authority in their area of expertise. Such authority—called staff or functional authority—permits the staff to issue instructions and directives in their area of expertise:

> In the pure staff situation, the advisors on personnel, accounting, purchasing, or public relations have no part of this (formal) authority, their duty being merely to offer counsel. But when the president delegates authority to these advisors to issue instructions directly to the line organization . . . that right is called "functional authority". . . . In virtually every larger enterprise, and in many smaller enterprises, some delegation of functional authority to staff departments seems unavoidable. . . . This practice is due largely to the necessity for expert interpretation of policy and for formulation of procedures by specialists, which in turn results from the need for varying degrees of uniformity in accounting, labor, public relations, and other activities.[25]

Functional authority does not carry the right to discipline, however. Compliance must still be sought by going through the line, thus preserving the unity of com-

---

[21] Brown (1960).

[22] Koontz and O'Donnell (1976), p. 332.

[23] Dalton (1959).

[24] Litterer (1973), p. 585.

[25] Koontz and O'Donnell (1976), pp. 342, 349.

mand, that is, one person, one boss.[26] This concept of functional or staff authority is now widely accepted, and research studies have attempted to examine how the functional authority of staff roles such as the controller and the personnel manager vary across specific areas of responsibility in actual practice.[27]

Some contemporary organizations have gone one step farther, having recognized the need for more than one formal chain of command when more than one point of focus is critical to the organization's success, for example, product *and* functional focus, line *and* staff focus. Organizations with two or more command systems are called "matrix" organizations.[28]

This review of the literature on line and staff points to one fundamental question that the organization must address: How will it ensure that the appropriate specialist knowledge, expertise, and judgment are brought to bear when decisions are made? With increasing organizational size and complexity, the importance of the specialist's contribution has increased, and organizations have tried to facilitate the incorporation of such input from the specialists by giving them greater functional authority. As Lawler and Rhode point out,

> The question of how staff jobs can be redesigned to improve the line/staff interface is difficult to answer. Essentially the issue is power. The staff wants more of it and the line resists giving it up. . . . Probably the most effective solution to the problem of line/staff conflict lies in giving the staff more formal decision-making power. In effect this means reducing the distinction between line and staff employees.[29]

But formal authority represents only one means by which staff employees can influence decisions.[30] Studies indicate how staff employees are able to influence many decisions whether or not they have formal authority.[31] In a study of 212 chief accountants in small-, medium-, and large-sized companies in the United Kingdom, McKenna[32] found that the chief accountant's relationship with managers in other functions was ill-defined and did not fit the stereotyped notion of the staff specialist acting in an advisory capacity. The chief accountant relied on a mixture of tactics—including persuasion and bargaining—to exert influence in matters con-

---

[26] Logan (1966); Brown (1960); Fisch (1961).

[27] Henning and Moseley (1970); French and Henning (1966).

[28] Davis and Lawrence (1977).

[29] Lawler and Rhode (1976), p. 189.

[30] The concepts of authority, power, and influence are closely related and are used interchangeably in common usage. They are defined as follows: authority is the *formal right* to act; power is the *ability* to act; and influence refers to the *process* of altering others' behavior, attitudes, or feelings (Filley, House, and Kerr, 1976).

[31] Pettigrew (1972); Crozier (1954).

[32] McKenna (1979).

nected with his or her role. Strauss[33] defined the effectiveness of purchasing agents in terms of their ability to develop political power and described the tactics used by them to enhance their influence within the organization. As McGregor pointed out many years ago,

> the conventional line-staff distinction in terms of authority is an illusion. The industrial organization is an elaborate complex of interdependent relationships, and interdependence means that each party can affect the ability of the other to achieve his goals and satisfy his needs.

> It is admittedly awkward and frustrating to be responsible for accomplishing objectives under conditions in which one cannot control the relevant factors in the situation. It would be much nicer if reality were different. However, given the complex interdependencies of modern society, we are often in such situations. . . . [For instance] management is responsible to the stockholders for the economic success of the enterprise. However, it cannot *control* consumers' preferences or their attitudes toward saving money or buying goods; the general economic health of the nation; legislation in municipal, state, or federal bodies; labor unions; or a host of other phenomena, including the behavior of subordinates within the organization. It can *influence* many of these determining variables; it cannot control them—especially in the narrow sense of exercising authority over them.[34]

In the same vein, Kotter[35] has argued that, although "power" and "influence" typically evoke negative reactions, managers need both to cope effectively with the dependencies inherent in their work. Echoing the same theme, Kanter[36] recently emphasized the importance of power and influence for staff personnel.

If the foregoing is a valid analysis, an important aspect of staff work is the ability to *influence* organizational decisions. Providing information and analysis of high quality—the "service" role of staff as traditionally conceived—is of little use if it does not get factored into the organizational decision-making process.

CONTROLLER INFLUENCE VERSUS INVOLVEMENT

Because power and influence are value-laden terms, it is difficult to measure them reliably. In the study of the purchasing agent's influence, for example, Strauss[37] relied not only on questionnaires and interviews but also on a considerable number of informal contacts, including direct observation of agents at work for periods up

---

[33] Strauss (1962).
[34] McGregor (1960), pp. 146, 158.
[35] Kotter (1977).
[36] Kanter (1979).
[37] Strauss (1962).

to one week. Such a methodology has the potential of yielding rich data and insights but is expensive and time consuming. It limits the number of cases that can be investigated within a given amount of time. The present study included a wide range of companies so it was difficult to examine any one in sufficient depth to make an assessment of the level of influence exerted. That is why an indirect indicator—the *degree of involvement* in decision making—is used.

In theory, the relationship between degree of involvement and influence is not a direct one. While those who influence decisions tend to be actively involved in the decision-making process, the opposite does not necessarily follow. It is possible for a person to be involved in decision making and yet have little or no influence on the decision in the sense of having an impact on the final choice. In practice, however, the two seem to go hand in hand. More of one is commonly associated with more of the other. While this assertion is not documented here, controllers actively involved in decision making also appeared to be influencing decisions. Because of the logical distinction between involvement and influence, however, and because no attempt was made to measure the latter with reliability, the findings are reported in terms of degree of involvement rather than the degree of influence.

CONTROLLER INVOLVEMENT VERSUS INDEPENDENCE

In addition to the responsibility for assisting management in the running of the business, requiring some degree of involvement in the decision-making process, the controller is responsible for accurate reporting of financial information to stockholders and government agencies and is also responsible for protection of the company's assets (see Exhibit 1-1 and items 1 and 2 in the related summary on page 8). The last two responsibilities are of a custodial and monitoring nature and require a degree of controller independence from management.

The question of controller independence is an important one from the standpoint of both society and the corporation. From society's standpoint, inaccurate reporting not only undermines public confidence in the corporation but also dampens efficient resource allocation. At the time of this writing, for example, one company disclosed an investigation into possible profit-juggling practices at certain operating units that may have had the effect of smoothing quarterly and yearly earnings to show steady growth.[38] Some securities analysts believe that the distortions could prove large enough to have misled the investors; that is, if the company's earnings weren't as smooth from quarter to quarter or from year to year as had been reported previously, the company may have been a riskier investment than investors were led to believe.

[38] "Initial Study of Some Heinz Units Finds $5.5 Million in Profit-Juggling Practices," *The Wall Street Journal*, July 2, 1979, p. 1; and "Slick Accounting Ploy Helps Companies Improve Their Income," *The Wall Street Journal*, June 20, 1980, p. 1.

From the corporation's standpoint, invalid reporting can distort resource allocation *within* the firm, leading to a less efficient deployment of corporate resources. In addition, matters concerning both reporting and internal control have gained a new urgency following enactment of the Foreign Corrupt Practices Act. Both companies and their executives are subject to civil and criminal liability for inaccurate reporting or failure to maintain an adequate system of internal controls.

Is the controller's responsibility for external reporting and custody of company assets, requiring a degree of independence from management, inconsistent with the responsibility for management service, requiring a degree of involvement in management? This is a critical question because both responsibilities are important for reasons given in the preceding sections. Can the controller wear these two hats effectively—one that of an umpire or police officer, the other that of a helper or counsellor?

Some have argued that the answer is no, that the helping role and the role of police officer are absolutely incompatible. To place an individual in the latter is to destroy the possibility of his or her occupying the former one successfully.[39]

Others, however, have taken the contrary position:

> the proposal to remove the internal auditing function from the controller's jurisdiction and set it up as a separate function is based on one or both of two lines of reasoning—first, that it is unsound for the controller to check his own work and, second, that internal auditing is a job which is likely to arouse the conscious or unconscious antagonism of the operating executives and therefore hamper the controller in his management service activities.

> The problem can be superficially solved by arbitrarily narrowing the range of responsibilities—in the controller's case by removing from his jurdisdiction all property-control and legal functions or even relieving him of any responsibility for designing and operating the basic accounting records. Such a course, however, has two disadvantages: first, it weakens the coordination of various phases of the same basic function, and, second, it complicates top management's problem by increasing the number of lines of responsibility at or near the top level.[40]

Another important disadvantage not mentioned is the *kind* of control that results when the controller's responsibility excludes management service. Without the opportunity for active involvement in business decision making that the service role provides, the controller may not be privy to sensitive management information and deliberations in progress. Thus, the controller's role becomes one of checking compliance with corporate policy and procedures after the relevant decisions have already been made, that is, *after-the-fact or reactive control.* In contrast, a controller actively involved with management in business decision making has an

---

[39] McGregor (1960), p. 169.
[40] Bradshaw and Hull (1950), pp. 103, 107.

opportunity to put an early stop to ill-conceived, ill-advised, or illegal courses of action being contemplated, that is, *before-the-fact or anticipatory control.* More responsive control is therefore possible with a broadened definition of the controller's areas of responsibility, *provided that the controller's involvement in management does not impair the controller's sense of objectivity and independence, or vice versa.*

The question of whether controller involvement adversely affects controller independence has relevance beyond the role of the controller. There are other staff groups, such as legal and personnel, where responsibilities for serving and monitoring management are *both* increasing in importance. On the one hand, because of increasing size and complexity, management needs to rely more heavily on the advice and expertise of these staffs. On the other hand, as the corporation experiences the pressures of our modern and increasingly regulated and litigious era, the monitoring role is also increasing in importance. For example, increased liability exposure makes legal questions more important; mounting equal employment opportunity claims make equity and fairness in personnel decisions more critical.

While acknowledging the need for better control of these and other activities, some would argue that the way in which to accomplish this is by holding the *general managers* accountable, not by having staff monitor these areas. The general managers are, of course, accountable to the corporate management and the board of directors for decisions affecting these and other areas of their responsibility. But corporate management and the boards are also accountable to the stockholders and the general public for corporate performance, and the liability exposure that such accountability entails has been on the rise.

Until recently, personal liability was limited to actions known to management and the board. Liability is now generally presumed to extend to matters that management and the board *should* have known about. The broader interpretation of culpability increases the importance of securing appropriate and valid information from lower management levels. Corporate management and the board may therefore seek a system of checks and balances in areas of particular concern to them. If this were not so, there would be no need for a corporate internal audit function, for instance. Many corporations chose to install such a function because of their particular concern with the maintenance of internal control.

However, even if the corporation has a strong internal audit staff at headquarters that periodically visits the field locations, this group cannot offer the *continuous* vigilance that the local controller can. Neither do corporate auditors typically have the depth of knowledge about local systems, people, and practices to be able to detect subtle misrepresentations or inadequacies. Thus, the corporation must rely on the local controller to be an effective local guardian.

Just as the corporate internal audit staff is not in as good a position as the local controller to provide continuous vigilance or to detect subtle misrepresentations at the local level, so too is the case for other staff positions such as personnel, legal, and quality control. As these other staff areas become of greater concern, corporate executives may seek a method of checks and balances in these areas as well.

Thus, the question of staff independence, and the related question of the relationship between involvement and independence, are of considerable practical significance. Although this is a book about the service role, specifically the degree of controller involvement in business decisions, there is an attempt to determine the extent to which such involvement affects other responsibilities requiring a degree of independence from management. The next chapter includes such an examination using the data available from this study. The broader question of how controller involvement affects other aspects of company performance is also explored.

chapter 2

Controller Involvement and Company Performance

This book is focused on controller involvement because its importance is evident from an examination of staff roles in general and that of the controller in particular, as discussed in the first chapter. But what precisely are the consequences of controller involvement for company performance?

The question is difficult to address for two reasons. First, which aspects of company performance should be considered? Second, controller involvement is only one of a multitude of factors influencing any single dimension of company performance. How can its influence be isolated?

In this chapter the following approach is adopted. The evidence on the association between controller involvement and company financial performance is first considered. Two questions concerning possible negative consequences are then examined: whether controller involvement stifles initiative and creativity of operating executives and whether involvement compromises controller independence. Finally, a framework that permits these issues to be related and reviewed in a broader context is presented.

The scheme, covering four basic "patterns" found among the companies studied, was not anticipated during data collection. Rather, these patterns emerged from an analysis of the data after the field work had been completed. The existence of these patterns is being *asserted* here on the basis of qualitative analysis and a clinical understanding of the companies studied. Their *testing* remains the province of future research. The case appendix at the end of this chapter illustrates each of the four basic patterns with prototypical cases.

CONTROLLER INVOLVEMENT
AND FINANCIAL PERFORMANCE

The association between financial performance and degree of controller involvement is positive—companies with higher degrees of typical division controller involvement have, in general, higher financial performance relative to the average of their industry.[1]

It is difficult to be sure about which is the cause and which is the effect in this relationship. Does higher company financial performance cause higher levels of controller involvement or is it the other way around? Although unable to *prove* it with the available data, the answer is probably *both*. The causality appears to flow in both directions, as described in the paragraphs that follow.

There are two reasons why higher financial performance leads to greater controller involvement. First, because of the absence of financial stress, top management is not continually engaged in obtaining performance information from the divisions or especially sensitive about its validity.[2] Under these conditions, the company's controllers are not preoccupied with their custodial and monitoring role and have time and energy to participate in business decisions. A second reason is that when financial performance is high, the company can afford the resources[3] needed to select, train, and develop controllers who can contribute actively in business decision making.

Although it is difficult to argue that controller involvement is the cause of higher company financial performance, the general opinion of the managers interviewed is that controller involvement does contribute to the "bottom line." These views are now described.

Areas of Contribution

In the initial field visits an attempt was made to obtain the opinions of general managers about the extent of their controllers' contributions to companys' profitability, but this approach did not work. These managers were unable or unwilling to quantify such contributions. An alternate, less direct, approach was tried in the later visits. General managers were asked the following question: "What difference, if any, can outstanding versus average controllers make in your company as far as the 'bottom line' [profitability] is concerned? Please indicate your best guess of the most likely impact on profits."

[1] For the 24 companies studied, the coefficient of correlation is 0.38. Had the companies been a statistical random sample (which they were not), this correlation would have been statistically significant at the 0.10 level. See variables D1 and Q7 in the Methodological Appendix for definition of the variables.

[2] Argyris (1953); Herman (1963).

[3] Theorists have coined the phrase "organizational slack" to describe the condition in which the organization has some "elbow room" in the area of availability of resources (Cyert and March, 1963).

There were three major types of responses. Sometimes the answer was "Zero percent. Controllers are staff executives; they do not contribute to profit." Most often managers answered with a figure greater than zero percent (the range was 0-25 percent, with an average value of 9 percent) but indicated that they were not confident of their estimate. Sometimes the response was "It is impossible to quantify the contribution." Whatever the response, the follow-up question asked was "[Whether or not you are able to quantify the contribution] can you give some examples of what types of controller contributions lead to a bottom-line impact?"

While the specific examples given varied, four major areas of contribution were commonly mentioned: control of receivables, inventories, operating expenses, and capital expenditures. Financial analysis, prevention of fraud, and management of taxes were also mentioned. If these are the principal areas of controller contribution to company profitability, the degree of importance of the controller's contribution depends on the degree to which these areas are critical for a given company. Results presented in Part II of this book do in fact indicate a weak positive association between capital asset intensity[4] and degree of corporate controller involvement at headquarters and a positive association between working asset intensity[5] and degree of typical division controller involvement.

Although higher capital asset and working asset intensity are generally associated with higher corporate and division controller involvement, there are exceptions. Given the importance of the controller's contribution in these areas, low controller involvement is particularly dysfunctional under conditions of high capital asset and working asset intensity. Interviews indicate considerable dissatisfaction with low involvement under these conditions. According to a senior executive at company 11, for instance. "Our controllers are good but not outstanding. They are cost oriented rather than people oriented. They are unable to challenge the line. Consequently, they have little impact on business decisions. The company *is* hurting because of this. No one says, 'Look, you said you were going to do X, but. . .'." The extent to which such expressed dissatisfaction reflects an actual performance loss for the company is unclear, but it seems likely that this company would benefit from greater controller involvement.

Although controller involvement does contribute to the bottom line, there are two possible negative consequences associated with it. The first of these is now considered.

DOES CONTROLLER INVOLVEMENT STIFLE MANAGEMENT CREATIVITY?

Since the essence of controller involvement is the recommending of courses of action and the challenging of plans and actions of operating executives, it is possible that such involvement stifles creativity and initiative of operating executives. As

---

[4] Variable D6 in the Methodological Appendix.
[5] Variable D7 in the Methodological Appendix.

one manager pointed out, "The weakness in this way of operating [high degree of controller involvement] is that at times it hinders real marketing creativity and entrepreneurship. There is a constant checkpoint and rein when the controller's advice is pitted against that of R&D, marketing, and sales." Another executive agreed that this was a potential problem, but added "Yes, horses can run faster without harness! Unfortunately, they may also run in the wrong direction or they may leave the wagon behind."

Because active controller involvement can result in important contributions for the company as just described, the interesting question is, Can controllers remain actively involved in business decisions without stifling the creativity and initiative of operating executives?

It seems that the answer is yes. The chemistry of the controller's interpersonal relationships with operating executives, particularly the level of interpersonal trust, is part of the answer. But the prevailing managerial attitudes and assumptions are also important. Where executives emphasize formal authority in their managerial approach, they are more likely to view active controller involvement as an "infringement" on their areas of authority and responsibility. Where the role of formal authority in organizational life is deemphasized, the actual danger of stifling managerial creativity and initiative is likely to be far less. The following case of a division of company 14 illustrates how active controller involvement can make a significant contribution in business decision making without stifling the creativity and initiative of operating executives.

Controller Involvement in a Division of Company 14

One of the most important activities in this division is the development and introduction of new products, which account for 20-30 percent of any given year's sales. According to the vice president of marketing, "With so many new products being introduced every year, profitability and cost forecasting are crucial." According to the division controller, "Which new products should we produce and sell? That's the key decision here. New product analysis requires coordination between R&D, marketing, manufacturing, and sales. Pricing strategy, advertising, and promotion must all be considered carefully. The typical lead time on new product introduction is a year and a half."

According to the division's general manager, "In new product development, there is a continuing issue about who plays what role to what extent. Each function feels that it should play the lead role. What tends to happen is that R&D takes the lead but the controller is deeply involved from the outset. He plays a very important role in the costing process and I rely very heavily on the information he provides me. The controller will come to me frequently to alert me, that is, 'Are you aware that . . .' or 'I am concerned about product X because . . .'. Early in new product development he may come to me and say 'R&D will tell you that the molds for that new product will cost $2.18 a piece. You ought to know there is no way in hell they will come that cheap. They will say we can buy it in Korea. But you don't want to buy in Korea because . . .'. The controller questions not only the VPs but questions me as well, both before *and after* action has been taken. He might say, for example, 'Look, I know you have done this, but let me show you something. . .'. The controller is my right-hand man because he can quickly grasp information of *real* concern to me. We respect and trust each other."

According to the division's vice president of operations, "It is the company's benefit to have a financial person on the management team who can be outspoken and play the questioning role. One can make the case that the division general manager should be the one doing this, but my experience has been that the DGM has his own preferences and biases. The financial guy is in a good position to provide a check on that. The approach has worked extremely well for us, as witnessed by our solid profitability and growth record."

CONTROLLER INVOLVEMENT
VERSUS INDEPENDENCE

The questionnaire data to be presented in Part II of this book indicate a negative association between management's expectations regarding controller involvement and their expectations concerning controller independence. The interviews also suggest that managers tend to view the controller's role of contribution to business decisions to be somewhat at odds with the custodial and monitoring role. As one chief financial officer pointed out, "If the controller becomes too involved in operating decisions, he loses his integrity and independence when offering the *financial* implications of operating decisions, that is, it is not clear to others if he is biasing the financial analysis to fit the operating position advocated by him. I don't want controllers to be business managers because of the trade-off [losing financial integrity versus contributing by involvement]." To what extent does controller involvement really compromise controller independence?

To address the question, a method is needed for determining the degree to which controller independence is in fact adversely affected by active controller involvement. There was no reliable basis for making such an assessment in this study. Beyond the difficulty of getting executives to talk about this sensitive topic is the more basic problem that executives themselves may not know if such compromises are occurring. They would like to believe that *no* such compromises are taking place. The best that could be done was to get executives to talk about whether serious compromises had actually come to light within the company in the *recent past*. Compromise of independence was considered to have occurred *if the local controller was partly blamed* for the following: fraud, defalcation, or illegal payments by company personnel and/or "accounting surprises" or "blowups," that is, large, *unexpected* write-offs of inventory and receivables. The following is a brief account of one of these incidents.

One general manager had gotten the company to commit large sums of money to increase capacity in anticipation of growth that was simply not being realized. To "buy time" the manager, in cooperation with the division controller, began "window dressing" the books. Bad debts were not being recognized whereas sales on backlog orders were being recorded. This went on for two years. The division controller then left and was never replaced. The manager kept saying he was still looking for an appropriate candidate to fill the important vacancy. Two more years went by before corporate executives finally discovered what was going on. A $3-million loss had to be absorbed immediately.

When instances of serious loss of controller independence such as these were compared with the degree of controller involvement, no pattern was evident. Of the nine instances of such loss of independence uncovered in this study, in four the local controller appeared to be actively involved in business decisions; in the other five, less so.

The question of controller independence is essentially a matter of personal integrity and professionalism. As in the case of the relationship between controller involvement and management creativity, however, the *way* in which the controller discharges his or her responsibilities, particularly the care taken to develop and maintain the respect and trust of associated operating executives, is important to the question of whether involvement inhibits independence. Effective behavior—in the sense of accomplishing involvement *and* independence—is illustrated with the following examples.

One apparently highly effective division controller stated the following: "I never call corporate headquarters to give them important information without first informing our management. If there is an unpleasant surprise, I always give my manager sufficient time to report up the line so *his* boss doesn't first find out from someone else. I lose my credibility with division management if I am viewed as a spy. I compromise my professional ethics if I don't keep corporate management informed. I must be firm but fair."

Said another division controller highly regarded by many, "I was with the company's external auditors before coming here in the early seventies. It took me a year to build up credibility. Management is typically concerned about forecast revisions and questions about reserves for bad debts and inventory obsolescence. I gained acceptance by getting to know the people and being judicious in communicating sensitive information. . . . Sometimes I have to put my foot down—for example, if there are potential legal questions concerning fair pricing or illegal buying practices. During the period of wage-price controls, for instance, our salespeople wanted to raise selling prices. I said no. They said others are doing it. I said, 'Then they are illegal. We are not going to be.'"

The way in which the corporate controller or group controllers deal with the division controller and division management also appears to be important if the division controllers are to retain independence while remaining involved. Said one corporate controller who received high marks from both the chief executive officer and division management, "To develop and nurture good relations, I visit the divisions as often as possible. Even if on vacation, I'll stop by and have dinner with the division controllers—I know 99 percent of the controllers, 60 percent of their spouses. When visiting field locations, I want to know about the *big* things, for example, inventory valuation, bad debt reserves, new product development costs. My auditing background has taught me how to try and find out what's *really* going on. I'll get to know the people and the problems over coffee, cocktails, dinner—whatever it takes. If there are problems, I encourage the controller and local management to themselves inform corporate management before I have to."

At another company, group controllers were used to facilitate the maintenance of objectivity and independence. One group controller in this company described his role as follows: "I am an ombudsman for the division controllers and buffer them from corporate headquarters. I understand their language and can act as a screen for them. One third of the time I can handle the information requested by corporate headquarters right here (myself). Other times, corporate is asking the wrong questions to get the information they need or there are multiple requests. I am the liaison for the divisions and interpret their position for corporate head-quarters. Among my specific responsibilities are standardization of policy, capital project review, and follow-up on negative audit reports." Again, the "watchdog role" of the group controllers was apparently made more tenable because they encouraged division management to themselves report the critical, sensitive information. According to the chief financial officer, "I have told the group controllers *never* to come to me with data that they haven't had a chance to send up through the line. *How* things get communicated is important. We use information with discretion."

As these last two examples illustrate, the question of whether controller involvement compromises independence cannot be answered adequately in isolation. The context is important, for example, the behavior of the corporate and group controllers in the two examples just cited. The same can be said about the earlier discussion on whether controller involvement stifles management initiative and creativity and whether involvement is related to financial performance. Controller involvement is only a piece of the puzzle. Other factors concurrently influence controller independence, management creativity, and company financial performance, making it very difficult to isolate the impact of controller involvement. If the broader context is considered, however, certain interesting "patterns" emerge. These patterns are now examined.

PATTERNS OF RISK TAKING, CONTROL, CONTROLLER INVOLVEMENT, AND PERFORMANCE

As mentioned previously, these patterns were not expected at the outset. Rather, they emerged from analyses of the data when attempting to assess the consequences of controller involvement. The existence of the patterns is being *asserted* here on the basis of qualitative analysis and clinical understanding of the companies studied. Their *testing* is left to future research.

Exhibit 2-1   Patterns of Risk Taking, Control, Controller Involvement, and Performance

		Degree of Risk Taking[a]	
		Low	*High*
Degree of Control[a]	*Low*	**Pattern 1** (Two companies) Low to moderate controller involvement Low financial performance Executives indicate that low control, controller involvement, and risk taking are "hurting" the company; recent incidents of accounting surprises	**Pattern 2** (Four companies) Low to moderate controller involvement High financial performance Executives indicate that low control and controller involvement are "hurting" the company; recent incidents of accounting surprises; management attempting to "upgrade" controllers.
	High	**Pattern 3** (Four companies) Moderate to high controller involvement Low financial performance Executives indicate that "stifled" initiative and creativity are "hurting" the company *Pattern 3A:* Situation attributed to legacy of near bankruptcy (two companies) *Pattern 3B:* Situation attributed to management's attitude and philosophy (two companies)	**Pattern 4** (Four companies) High controller involvement High financial performance Executives indicate none of the adverse consequences mentioned in patterns, 1, 2, and 3

[a]These terms are defined below.

Because it was neither planned to examine these patterns when undertaking the study nor were they anticipated during the field work, the data to be presented are spotty. Only 14 of the 24 companies in the study could be classified into the four basic patterns shown in Exhibit 2-1. The two major dimensions of the classification scheme are defined as follows:

> *Degree of risk taking* denotes the extent to which risk taking is evident in *management's* attitudes and actions.

Degree of control denotes the extent to which *management* is consistently able to meet predetermined performance targets.

A company was classified as high on degree of risk taking if there appeared to be some consensus among those interviewed that the company's management was "risk taking," "aggressive," or "entrepreneurial." On the other hand, if there was some consensus that management was "risk averse," "cautious," or "conservative," the company was classified as low on degree of risk taking. In all other cases the company was not classified on the risk-taking dimension.

A company was classified as high on degree of control if there appeared to be some consensus among those interviewed that the company's management was able to consistently meet predetermined performance targets. If, on the contrary, there was some consensus among those interviewed that the management was frequently unable to meet projected performance targets, the company was classified as low on degree of control. In all other cases the company was not classified on the control dimension.

The classification procedure explains why only 14 of the 24 companies in the study could be classified on both the risk taking and control dimensions. To repeat, the study of these dimensions, particularly the degree of risk taking, had not been planned. Thus no attempt was made during the field work to systematically assess a company's position on these dimensions. However, 14 of the 24 companies could be classified on the two dimensions because of consensus in the interview data.

It should be noted that this classification scheme is not based directly on the degree of *controller* involvement within the company. However, four revealing patterns emerge when the degree of risk taking, control, controller involvement, and company performance are considered together. The distinguishing characteristics of each of these basic patterns are now described.

Pattern 1: Low Risk Taking, Low Control

These companies appeared to be "hurting" on account of the low degree of control in general and the low degree of controller involvement in particular (Exhibit 2-2). It was difficult to attribute specific consequences to the latter because it was one aspect of the former. However, the performance consequences identified appeared to be dysfunctional.

Risk taking was not evident in these companies. It was not clear to what extent this was responsible for the poor financial performance of these companies. In one case (company 11) recent divestiture of "bad" acquisitions was mentioned as a reason for the poor financial performance. No such reasons were apparent in the other case (company 22).

Finally, the phrases "egomaniac" or "egotistical" were used to describe a key actor in each of these companies—the current chair (previous chief executive officer) of company 11 and the current chair and chief executive officer at com-

Exhibit 2-2 Pattern 1: Low Risk Taking, Low Control[a]

Company[b]	Degree of Typical Division Controller Involvement[c]	Degree of Corporate Controller Involvement at Headquarters[d]	Financial Performance Relative to Average of Company's Industry[e]	Other Performance Consequences
11	Moderate	Moderate	Considerably below average	Executives indicate that low control, risk taking, and controller involvement are "hurting" the company
22	Low	Moderate	Considerably below average	Same indications as above and recent incidents of accounting surprises and fraud

[a]These terms are defined on page 28.
[b]Exhibit 3-5 contains background information on the companies.
[c]See variable Q7 in the Methodological Appendix.
[d]Variable Q6.
[e]Variable D1.

pany 22. Company executives attributed management's cautious attitude and general "weakness" to this "egomania" syndrome. The characteristics of pattern 1 companies are illustrated with one prototypical case—company 22—included in the Case Appendix at the end of this chapter.

Pattern 2: High Risk Taking, Low Control

As with pattern 1 companies, these companies also appeared to be suffering the consequences of a low degree of control in general and a low degree of controller involvement in particular (Exhibit 2-3). Again, it was difficult to attribute specific performance consequences to one versus the other, but they appeared to be dysfunctional.

Unlike pattern 1 companies, the management of these companies placed a great deal of emphasis on risk taking. These companies had grown by acquiring businesses owned by independent entrepreneurs, and management seemed preoccupied with maintaining the "entrepreneurial spirit." It was not clear to what extent such entrepreneurship contributed to the uniformly high financial performance of these companies (company 9 was the only instance of average performance).

In three of the four companies, management was seeking ways of increasing the degree of controller involvement without stifling risk taking. At company 16 no such effort was underway, but some executives were concerned about the potential for trouble inherent in the low current emphasis on control. The characteristics of pattern 2 companies are illustrated with one prototypical case—company 21—included in the Case Appendix at the end of this chapter.

Pattern 3A: Low Risk Taking, High Control—The Legacy of Near Bankruptcy

Unlike pattern 1 and 2 companies, pattern 3 companies had a high degree of control and moderate to high degrees of controller involvement. They were not plagued by the control problems experienced by companies in patterns 1 and 2 (Exhibit 2-4).

Two pattern 3 companies had verged on bankruptcy within one generation of the current management. These companies—pattern 3A—had several executives who were concerned that management's continuing preoccupation with control was stifling risk taking. Thus, while it was easy to attribute the poor financial performance of these companies to the near bankruptcy and its aftermath, it was difficult to assess to what extent the apparent stifling of creativity and initiative had adversely affected company performance. The Case Appendix includes a description of a prototypical pattern 3A company—company 8—how this company was led to near bankruptcy, the recovery process, and the consequences of the traumatic legacy.

Exhibit 2-3 Pattern 2: High Risk Taking, Low Control[a]

Company[b]	Degree of Typical Division Controller Involvement[c]	Degree of Corporate Controller Involvement at Headquarters[d]	Financial Performance Relative to Average of Company's Industry[e]	Other Performance Consequences
9	Moderate	No data	Average	Executives indicate that low control and controller involvement are hurting the company; recent incidents of accounting surprises and fraud; management attempting to "upgrade" controllers
16	Moderate	Low	Considerably above average	Executives concerned about possible problems with low control
21	Moderate	Low	Considerably above average	Recent incidents of accounting surprises; management attempting to "upgrade" controllers
24	Moderate	High	Considerably above average	Executives indicate that low controller involvement is "hurting" the company; management attempting to "upgrade" controllers

[a]These terms are defined on page 28.
[b]Exhibit 3-5 contains background information on the companies.
[c]See variable Q7 in the Methodological Appendix.
[d]Variable Q6.
[e]Variable D1.

Exhibit 2-4 Pattern 3: Low Risk Taking, High Control[a]

Company[b]	Degree of Typical Division Controller Involvement[c]	Degree of Corporate Controller Involvement at Headquarters[d]	Financial Performance Relative to Average of Company's Industry[e]	Other Performance Consequences
Pattern 3A: The Legacy of Near Bankruptcy				
8	High	Moderate	Below average	Executives indicate that "stifled" initiative and creativity are "hurting" the company
20	High	Moderate	Below average	Same as above
Pattern 3B: Risk-Averse Management Using Tight Controls				
2	High	Moderate	Below average	Executives indicate that management's risk aversion is "hurting" the company
15	Moderate	Moderate	Average	Executives indicate that "stifled" initiative and creativity are "hurting" the company

[a]These terms are defined on page 28.
[b]Exhibit 3-5 contains background information on the companies.
[c]See variable Q7 in the Methodological Appendix.
[d]Variable Q6.
[e]Variable D1.

Pattern 3B: Low Risk Taking, High Control—The Effects of Management's Attitude and Philosophy

These companies had many of the same attributes as the pattern 3A companies (Exhibit 2-4). A major difference was that management's preoccupation with control could not be attributed to the experience of a traumatic event such as a bankruptcy. Rather, it seemed to be related to management's attitude (risk averse) and philosophy (tight control). Pattern 3B companies are illustrated with the case of company 15 included in the Case Appendix.

Pattern 4: High Risk Taking, High Control

Pattern 4 companies had no control problems of the type encountered in patterns 1 and 2—these companies had high degrees of control and high degrees of controller involvement (Exhibit 2-5). Further, executives in these companies did not indicate absence of risk taking as did those in pattern 3—companies that also had high degrees of control. Pattern 4 companies had uniformly high financial performance as compared with the low financial performance of pattern 3 companies.

Although the difference in financial performance between patterns 3 and 4 cannot be attributed directly to the differences in perceived risk taking, one thing seems clear: if a high degree of control can be achieved without executives feeling "stifled" (pattern 4), this is preferable to the situation in which control is maintained but executives perceive a loss of the entrepreneurial spirit (pattern 3).

The pattern 4 companies are now illustrated with one prototypical case—company 14—to give the reader a flavor for how these companies perform the neat trick of achieving high degrees of risk taking *and* control. The case description indicates how a high degree of control is interrelated with active controller involvement and how high degrees of both control and controller involvement do not necessarily stifle initiative or creativity. The keys to overcoming the apparent dilemma appear to lie in the *way* in which risk taking is encouraged and control is achieved, particularly the emphasis that executives place on developing and maintaining a high level of interpersonal trust and respect while challenging each other to excel.

Company 14: A Prototype Case of Pattern 4

The controllers of this company were actively involved at both the corporate and the division levels. They were highly regarded within the company and appeared to be making a substantial contribution without stifling management creativity or initiative. According to a group vice president, "Our controllers rate 9 to 10 on a ten-point scale. They are actively involved and get behind the numbers. Basically what I do in my job is ask a lot of questions. Our controllers are so good that they have already asked those questions and have gotten the answers. For ex-

Exhibit 2-5   Pattern 4: High Risk Taking, High Control[a]

Company[b]	Degree of Typical Division Controller Involvement[c]	Degree of Corporate Controller Involvement at Headquarters[d]	Financial Performance Relative to Average of Company's Industry[e]	Other Performance Consequences
10	High	High	Above average	Executives indicate none of the adverse consequences mentioned in patterns 1, 2, and 3
14	High	High	Considerably above average	Same as above
18	High	High	Considerably above average	Same as above
23	High	High	Considerably above average	Same as above

[a]These terms are defined on page 28.
[b]Exhibit 3-5 contains background information on the companies.
[c]See variable Q7 in the Methodological Appendix.
[d]Variable Q6.
[e]Variable D1.

ample, the price of soybeans has gone up. My question is, 'If price has gone up, what's happening to margins?' The controller says 'There is no immediate impact because we own a soybean contract' and tells me when the contract runs out. We ask our controllers to be businessmen. It goes back to top management's philosophy."

According to the chief executive officer, "Controllers must be devil's advocates. To be effective, credibility is crucial. The track record will show if their judgments are good. In a crisis, they must be steady and calm, not capricious. There must be no flaps and they must get the facts." According to the chief operating officer, "The line executives in this company are financially oriented. I spend a lot of time with numbers and the controller is a trusted partner." According to the chief financial officer, "In this company, the controller is a *key* part of the management team. He is the eyes, ears, and sense of management. To be effective, he must not only be good at accounting, but he must be able to deal with people. People have to trust him and keep him super well informed. He must have breadth in his thinking."

Controllers commented on their own involvement as follows. According to a corporate assistant controller, "There is strong support for the control function at very senior levels in this company. Top management is responsible and *wants* control. They support strong controllership." According to a group controller, "A division controller's major responsibility is to be the general manager's alter ego. He must mentally make the same decisions the GM makes—he has the same information, data, and contacts as the GM. He must provide the GM with information even before the GM realizes the need for it. He must be a sounding board and open up communications. The controller who sticks with numbers and adopts the attitude 'that's none of my business—I am here to guard the company's assets' is going to be a failure."

Not only are controllers actively involved, the company has highly responsive controls. According to the chief executive officer, "We have one of the best early warning systems anywhere." According to the chief operating officer, "We operate in reasonably volatile markets and need to be quite responsive. We need extremely good knowledge—not only what happened and why, but *what's likely to happen*." According to a group vice president, "Our divisions inform us the minute there is a possibility of something's going wrong. Our controls are so good, I'd know the following immediately: 'here's what, here's why, here's what we are doing about it.' The divisions are evaluated on statistical yardsticks such as volume, market share, working capital, and new product development. The DGM is evaluated not only on the division's performance but also on leadership and ability to *anticipate* and respond."

Despite the strong controls and the high degree of controller involvement, there were no indications of "stifled" initiative or creativity. Rather, there was strong consensus among those interviewed about the excellent balance between risk taking and control. According to a division general manager, "There is a superb balance between control and risk taking in this company." According to the treasurer, "We work very closely with line management and provide continuing education to help them understand the financial mumbo jumbo, for example, senior executive conferences using du Pont's financial series. The pendulum is in just the right position between finance and marketing in this company. In a marketing division of our company (no sales, distribution, manufacturing), everything comes down to a number. In that case, the division general manager and the division controller are both pushing numbers. They work closely and in tandem. In the operating divisions, with all functions represented, the controller is typically the number 2 position. . . . If a company has a weak division controller or a weak division general manager, that spells trouble. If both are weak, that's dynamite in the house. The controller and the manager must both be strong." According to the assistant corporate controller, "The pendulum has swung to just the right point between control and creativity here."

According to the chief executive officer, "It is the *culture* we have here that makes it possible to operate as we do." According to the chief operating officer, "This is an informal company. Someone who prevents one from talking to others would be suspect. My boss, for example, goes and talks to my subordinates. I'm *glad.* Maybe he picked up some important information I don't have. We rely on a large number of different sources of information." According to the corporate controller, "A friend in another billion-dollar company once asked me to help him with a control problem they had. I said, 'Your philosophy is with numbers, ours is with people. I can't help you.' . . . This is a very humane company. We value our employees. We don't dismiss people without very careful consideration; but we do it when it is deserved."

This particular "culture" and "philosophy" was inculcated by the previous chief executive officer who diversified the company in the early 1960s. According to an account in the business press, "With any new acquisition, [the chief executive officer] installs his own controller in the company and monitors financial performance closely. Yet among new acquisitions and existing divisions alike, [he] favors an almost totally autonomous division management. He backs that up with a corporate emphasis on warm, relaxed, and low-key personal relations. When chatting with any of his divisional executives [the chief executive officer] conveys the impression that there is nothing he would rather do than share that particular conversation."

An important reason for the company's success in achieving high controller involvement without stifling operating executives appears to be the way in which the company's controllers have been trained and developed over the years. According to the assistant corporate controller, "A lot of us here, including most of the group controllers and many of the division controllers, were trained by the corporate controller. He taught us not to offer just numbers and analysis, but recommendations as well."

According to the corporate controller, "We don't feel that the controller's job is done when the accounting is done. We expect our controllers to be an integral part of the management team and continually challenge management. Individual professionalism, capability, and credibility are the keys. Credibility is earned over time, by being right in a technical and operating sense. It is important not to infringe on management's prerogative, so the *chemistry* of challenging, that is, the *way* the controller challenges and gets his point across, is critical. . . . We have relied primarily on in-house development for our controllers. We recruit capable individuals and bring them up against our strong group controllers and assistant controllers. We have had the greatest success with young people who not only have technical competence but maturity as well. Some work experience helps develop maturity. So does early participation in athletics, where one learns how to be a team player, what it means to win and lose, and how to fight back. These are important qualities of strong controllers."

According to the executive devoting full time to development of controllership personnel, "We don't have a formal training program. As young people come in, we watch them closely and categorize them as follows: (1) superstars or potential superstars—those with a proven track record of being able to get things done and displaying leadership, (2) very good performers—advancement probable, and (3) good performers but advancement unlikely."

The importance of the corporate controller's contribution to the company over the past three decades is captured by this comment made by the chief executive officer: "One of the most important decisions I will make if I live to be 65 is the choice of a successor to our corporate controller when he retires in a few years. He will be hard to replace."

Conclusion

The discussion and illustrations presented in this chapter suggest that, although the magnitude cannot be determined precisely, controller involvement does make an important contribution toward improving company performance. The potential problems associated with active controller involvement—loss of controller independence or the stifling of management creativity and initiative—are overcome if controllers and other managers are able to create and maintain interpersonal trust and respect while challenging each other to excel. The attitudes and skills that executives need to accomplish this are discussed in Part III of the book.

The illustrative material presented in this chapter also indicates that a variety of contextual factors, such as the company's environment and business conditions, management's orientation and operating style, and the company's approach to the training and development of its controllers, all influence the degree of controller involvement. The extent of such influence is examined more systematically in Part II of the book.

Readers not interested in a detailed examination of how and why various contextual factors influence the degree of controller involvement may wish to skip Part II and proceed directly to Part III dealing with the implications of the study for theory (Chapter 7) and practice (Chapter 8). These readers may wish to consult Exhibit 4-7 for a summary of how various contextual factors influence the degree of corporate controller involvement at headquarters. The analogous results for the degree of typical division controller involvement in the company are in Exhibit 6-4.

Those proceeding to Part II should be prepared for a dramatic change in the tone of the presentation. Hypotheses describing the influence of various contextual factors on controller involvement are developed, the underlying rationale is explained, and the statistical results are presented. This makes the reading "heavier" than in Part I; the discussion and presentation are more formal and quantitative. Illustrations are included from time to time to lighten the reading, but the reader should be prepared for slower progress.

Case Appendix

CASES ILLUSTRATING PATTERNS 1, 2,
AND 3 (EXHIBIT 2-1)

Company 22: A Prototypical Case
of Pattern 1 Companies

In the past, this company's strategy was based on quality and delivery ("We are the Cadillac of our industry"). Costs were less important because prices were only a secondary basis for competition. After the energy crisis of 1973, however, a softening of demand led to price cutting and resultant pressure on costs. Control of inventories, receivables, and manufacturing costs became much more important. The executives interviewed felt that more active controller involvement was needed under these conditions. According to a division general manager, "The division controller should provide a check on the operating executives, particularly those in marketing."

According to the budget analyst. "The divisions set their goals—they are not negotiated. Every other month a forecast is prepared for the remainder of the year, but no one questions achievement with respect to the previous forecast. On capital expenditures, there is no overall review by corporate staff. Only the chief executive officer reviews it."

According to the new chief financial officer, "We need to improve the integrity of our accounting system and to be more responsive. Financial control should be one of anticipation rather than response. Our bimonthly forecasts are off 20-40 percent. The budgets and capital requests are prepared without corporate staff involvement and review."

40

One set of consequences that some attributed to "weak" controllers (that is, controllers unable to challenge operating executives and recommend action) were two large, unexpected write-offs of inventory and receivables in two divisions of the company.

Several company executives attributed the company's problems in general to a conservative management dominated by a chief executive officer who apparently had run the company as a "one-man show" for over a decade. According to one senior executive, "The company remained dominated by the family until the founder died in the early 1950s. Since then the family influence has diminished, but the family still owns about 20 percent of the stock. The current management (all professionals) are very conservative. They are proud of the strong balance sheet."

Said another operating executive, "'The chief executive officer runs the company with a heavy hand. He is a dictator. He tried having a president under him four or five years ago. It didn't work. We haven't had a president since then."

According to a financial executive, "He is a competent businessman with a powerful personality—strong willed and egotistical. He feels that he knows more about finance than he actually does."

According to another financial executive, "We have had four chief financial officers in the last six years! After the last one left three years ago, the post remained vacant for a year and a half! A *lawyer* filled in as chief financial officer before the current chief financial officer was recruited from the outside last year. The instability and absence of financial leadership at the top of this company have contributed to many of its problems."

According to one senior manager, "The chief executive officer is opinionated and has reserved finance unto himself. He has no outside interests. This is the only life he knows. He is past retirement but isn't ready to step down. Sometimes he says he wants to leave but at other times he talks about how some division managers have a long way to go, and why he needs to be around a little longer. If he doesn't step aside soon he will lose some people who have been waiting in the wings."

Said another, "There is a missing generation of management here. The average age of our key management group is in the mid-40s—all of them were brought up by the chief executive officer. He made their careers. They are waiting for him to retire."

Company 21: A Prototypical Case
of Pattern 2 Companies

This company grew by acquiring independent businesses in the 1960s and early 1970s. Acquisitions were made only if the local management would stay on and if their attitude was consistent with that of the company's management. The emphasis on entrepreneurship is evident in this comment by the chief executive officer: "The people who run the different businesses of the company are individual businessmen. In effect, I am managing a portfolio of companies. We are a central bank. We do rely on group vice presidents to maintain control. . . . My major concern in this job is to keep track of people—very few people can perform well in the kind of unstructured environment we have. The GVPs stimulate and cultivate the people in the divisions."

The group vice presidents had no assigned staff to help them analyze the financial information. They relied on the thin corporate staff instead. According to one group vice president, "I get deeply involved in any crisis that occurs in my divisions. I demand much more information. The division manager steers the bicycle, but I help him pump. If the division manager is old and weak, I will even help him steer."

Thus, by visiting field locations the group vice presidents provided an element of control in the company. Said the chief executive officer, "Frequent visits permit visual control in addition to the monitoring of key numbers."

At the time of the research visit, corporate management was concerned about the adequacy of its system of control. According to a group vice preisdent, "When there are 'blowups' or accounting surprises, we replace the division general manager and/or the division controller. But similar problems crop up again. Maybe the problems relate more to our method of control than to the personalities of the people in question."

In response to these problems the company had recently decided to upgrade the salary levels of the controllers from $20,000 plus (with about a 20 percent bonus) to $30,000 plus with a 20 percent bonus in an attempt to attract more qualified people in the future and better motivate those already on board. A new corporate controller was hired from the outside, a controller's conference was being planned, and corporate executives were preparing job descriptions indicating what they expected of the division controllers and had asked the division general managers to do likewise. Both corporate and division management were concerned about whether the increased emphasis on more active division controller involvement would stifle the company's entrepreneurial spirit.

Company 8: A Prototypical Case of Pattern 3A Companies

The previous chief executive officer had built this company about equally from internal development and from acquisitions. He believed strongly in hiring young professional managers and in giving them plenty of latitude. By the early 1970s the company was large and diversified. Problems arose when unrelated businesses were acquired. According to the head of internal audit, "In those days, there were no approval and review procedures to speak of. No effective controls. Top management heard what they wanted to hear—good news only. They were not getting quality information. Sometimes the financial information provided by the newly acquired divisions was misleading if not completely fallacious. Top management was, however, too busy in further acquisitions." According to a group controller, "The previous chief executive officer was a 'hands-off' manager. . . . We had some controllers who were bookkeepers. False reporting, and lack of ability to report in some instances, led to the crisis."

This group controller went on to comment on the recovery process: "The current chief executive officer who took over is a 'hands-on,' financially oriented manager. The current chief financial officer took over then as the corporate controller. I was made an 'industry coordinator.' One of our first jobs was to assess the strength of the division controllers. Over the years the other group controllers and I have upgraded the quality of our division controllers dramatically by picking the best candidates for new appointments."

According to the director of budgets, "The financial orientation of the chief executive officer, and a strong chief financial officer, encouraged the development of strong controllers here. That's the demand side of the question. The supply side was tougher. It took two or three years before they found the right persons to be division controllers."

According to the chief financial officer. "When the financial crisis hit, the most critical piece of information I had to have was cash flow. The worst thing we could do was not perform on our obligations (interest and other payments due). I had inherited the planning function and had decided to convert the planning staff into industry coordinators. We had over a dozen of them, one for each industry we were in. Their job was to visit operations in their particular industry and give us the *facts*. It was a tough assignment, but every one knew that we needed good financial information to have a chance to avoid Chapter XI. We satisfied our lenders and gained credibility in six months. And we matured 15 years in 2 years."

In a memo to all staff department heads, including the corporate controller (current chief financial officer) soon after the crisis had been averted, the chief executive officer stated, "Given the dramatic change in the company during the past year, it is time for us to reevaluate the strategy of our staff/support functions. . . . My philosophy regarding staff support functions is that you should establish corporate policy and then monitor the entire corporate effort in your functional areas, subject to my approval where necessary. . . . You might consider the following steps: (1) Evaluate each function in terms of where, how, and why it is being performed. Compare the cost of a function against the value received. (2) Develop an organizational plan for the corporatewide organization of your functional area. (3) Develop plans and programs to increase the effectiveness of your functions."

According to the chief operating officer, "Staff strategies are less precise than are business strategies. But they do articulate, as well as is possible, what we want to accomplish in staff areas. By putting these goals in a descending order of priority, the staff strategy provides a framework for lopping off some priorities. This aids us in making good judgments, we hope."

Some executives were concerned that the "hands-on" management and strong controls that saved the company from bankruptcy were now stifling management initiative. According to one division general manager, "The previous chief executive officer gave a hell of a lot of latitude to the divisional general managers, with loose controls. As the company grew, he didn't know what was going on. Now, we have gone too far in the other direction. The current chief executive officer believes very strongly in staff—to the detriment of the line manager. In line-staff disputes, he tends to lean toward the staff."

Said another, "There has been a definite shift toward control since the crisis. There is less trust with the line manager. If this keeps up, we will become like one of our competitors (mentions company X)—ponderous, slow in decision making, managers who can't think for themselves and prisoners of policies and procedures."

Company 15: A Prototypical Case
of Pattern 3B Companies

The controllers in this company were actively involved in business decisions, and several company executives were concerned that the "pendulum had swung too far" toward finance and control. According to the vice president of corporate development, "There is a strong bias toward finance and control because there are several top executives here with a financial background." According to the vice president of corporate planning. "The pendulum may have swung too far toward control." According to the vice president of investor and bank relations, "Finance and control have increased in importance over the years. Today, it overpowers operations and marketing."

Further indication of the power of finance and control in this company is provided by the high degree of influence exercised by the corporate controller. Said the chief executive officer, "The corporate controller deals directly with the divisions and may intervene on issues such as advertising, intercompany pricing, payment of dividends by overseas subsidiaries, administrative fees, and so on." According to the corporate controller, "I have an excellent rapport with the division managers. This is important because I need to deal with them quite often, and credibility is critical when you are dealing with issues which affect divisional earnings."

There were indications that top management attitude was responsible for the low degree of risk taking. According to one senior executive, "We have a risk-averse management. Risk taking is low partly because the chief executive officer is close to retirement. He doesn't want to spoil his track record. . . . One of our shortcomings is that return on investment has not become a cornerstone of our management system. Management will talk about its importance, but it is not really used. Nobody is measured on it."

Another indication of management's risk-averse attitude came from a marketing consultant who had worked for a number of the company's major competitors: "This company's management is conservative to a fault."

part II

Contextual Factors and Controller Involvement

Part I of this book points to a variety of factors that influence the degree of controller involvement. In Part II the question of why and to what extent some of these factors are related to controller involvement is explored more systematically. Not all the relevant factors are examined, so it is important to be clear at the outset about which ones are considered and why.

Exhibit II-1 shows the three major classes of factors that Part I suggests are relevant in understanding and explaining variation in degree of controller involvement: (1) those related to the controller's motivation, personality, and interpersonal relationships with management; (2) those related to management's expectations, orientation, and operating philosophy; and (3) those related to characteristics of the company's environment and business. The last two classes of factors may be considered "contextual" in that they are not related to the *controller* but rather to the controller's *position.* Another way to state the distinction is that, were the controller to be replaced, the factors in class 1 would most likely change but those in classes 2 and 3 would not. It is these last two groups of factors that are the principal focus in Part II of this book. The basic research question addressed is this: Quite apart from the influence of the controller's motivation, personality, and the quality of his or her interpersonal relationships with management, what is the influence of the company's environment and business and of management's expectations, orientation, and operating philosophy, on the degree of controller involvement?

Such an exploration may be conducted by testing hypotheses derived from earlier work on the relationships between contextual factors and controller involvement. With the exception of the influence of management's expectations, however,

Exhibit II-1   Factors Influencing Controller Involvement

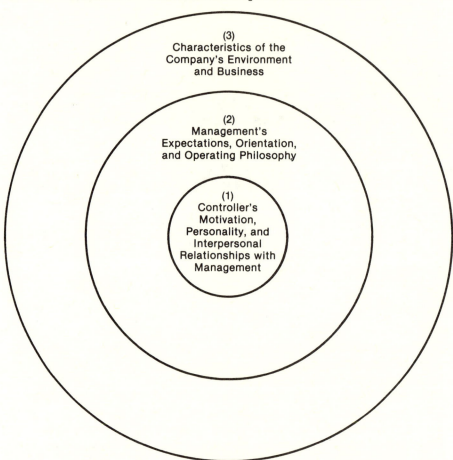

Part II of the book deals with factors in classes 2 and 3 only, that is, the "contextual" factors.

such work has not been done. Accordingly, the approach taken here is to draw on relevant theory to define the *domain* of the investigation, that is, the particular characteristics of the company's environment, business, and management selected for investigation. Specific hypotheses are then *developed* and *examined* with the available data. The *testing* of these hypotheses is left to future research. Thus, the statistical results that are presented constitute *exploratory* data analysis rather than *confirmatory* data analysis more commonly used in research. This study is concerned with hypotheses *generation,* not classical hypothesis *testing.*[1]

[1] In *The Discovery of Grounded Theory,* Glaser and Strauss (1967) comment at length on the bias in favor of theory verification and hypotheses testing in much social science research. They argue for the need for greater emphasis on theory generation and hypothesis formation.

Examination of the generated hypotheses indicates that several contextual factors are related to the degree of controller involvement. These results provide support for the "contingency" or "situational" perspective on organizational behavior because they indicate that controller involvement is contingent or dependent on the situation or the context in which the controller operates. However, the results also suggest that the current situational or contingency theories may have underestimated the important influence of management's expectations, orientation, and operating philosophy on organizational behavior. These management characteristics—the class 2 factors in Exhibit II-1—are more strongly related to controller involvement than are characteristics of the organization's environment or business—the class 3 factors in Exhibit II-1. Yet it is the latter set that receives the greatest attention in situational theories; the influence of the former has all too often been ignored. The implications of these results for development of theory and future research are considered in Part III (Chapter 7).

A schematic of the organizational territory covered in Part II is shown in Exhibit II-2. Following a description of the conceptual framework and methodology used to direct this research (Chapter 3), attention is turned to a study of how various contextual factors are related to the corporate controller's involvement at headquarters (Chapter 4). Several hypotheses are formulated and examined with the available data, and this permits the development of a descriptive model linking

Exhibit II-2 Schematic of Organizational Territory Covered in Chapters 4, 5, and 6

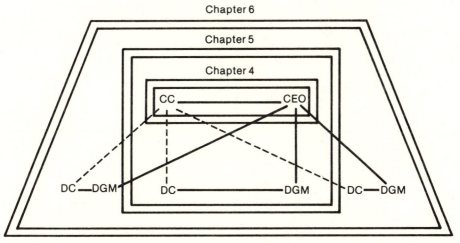

Nomenclature:

CEO - Chief executive officer————Direct reporting relationship
CC - Corporate controller- - - - - -Division controllers typically
DGM - Division general manager   report directly to their division
DC - Division controller   general managers, with a technical
                                                    or "dotted line" responsibility
                                                    to the corporate controller

various contextual factors to the corporate controller's involvement at head-quarters.

The hypotheses developed in Chapter 4 are reexamined in Chapter 5 with analogous data on the division controller's involvement within a business unit or division of the company. As Exhibit II-2 indicates, division controller involvement is influenced not only by the local management and business conditions but also by corporate management's relationship with the division. The influence of these factors is explored in Chapter 5.

This leads to a "top-down" perspective on the degree of typical division controller involvement in the company (Chapter 6), that is, a study of top management's influence on the degree of involvement of the company's division controllers in general. What these controllers have in common are the corporate controller, the corporate management, and the corporate context, and Chapter 6 explores the question of how these corporate contextual factors affect the typical level of division controller involvement in the company. In keeping with the format of Chapters 4 and 5, hypotheses are developed and examined in Chapter 6 and a descriptive model linking corporate contextual factors to the degree of typical division controller involvement in the corporation is constructed.

chapter 3

Conceptual Framework and Research Methodology

Before describing the conceptual framework and research methodology used here, its scope and limitations are discussed and the organizational arena of the investigation is more carefully specified.

SCOPE AND LIMITATIONS

Several steps were taken to limit the scope of the study and keep the project manageable. First, only U.S. corporations and their domestic divisions are included in this investigation. Second, the study is limited to large, multidivisional industrial firms—those with annual revenues in excess of $300 million. Finally, the focus is on controllers at senior levels in these companies. A description of the typical organization of these firms is now presented to specify the controller positions studied.

The Organizational Setting

A schematic of the organizational territory of interest is shown in Exhibit 3-1. At the corporate headquarters, the controller typically reports to the company's top financial executive (frequently called "chief financial officer" or "vice president of finance") who in turn reports to the company's chief executive officer. Thus, the corporate controller is generally one level removed from the chief executive officer in terms of the formal reporting relationship. But, because the chief financial officer normally has a wide range of responsibilities (treasurership, acquisitions, etc.), the chief executive office and those reporting directly to that position ("top management") often deal directly with the corporate controller in matters

49

concerning his or her areas of responsibility, for example, general accounting, cost accounting, taxes, internal audit, budgets and forecasts, financial analysis, and systems and procedures. Data processing reports either to the corporate controller or to the chief financial officer. Long-range planning typically reports to the chief financial officer or the chief executive officer.

Exhibit 3-1   The Typical Organizational Setting

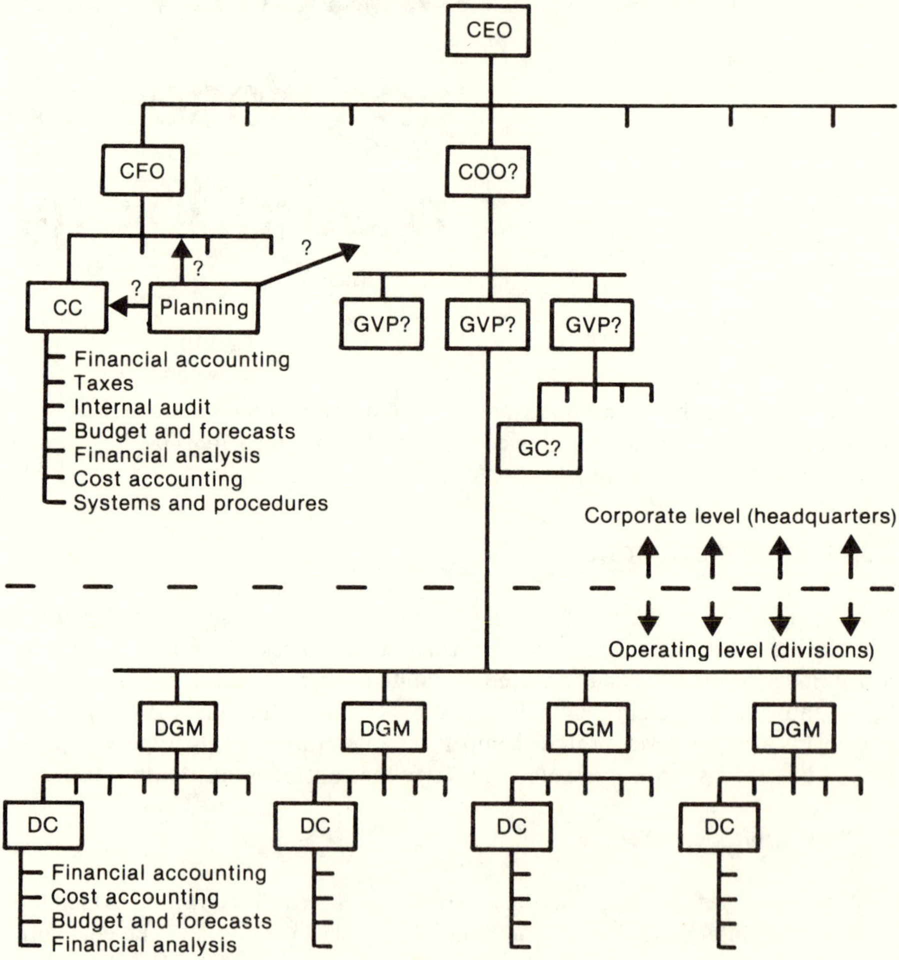

Nomenclature:

CEO - Chief executive officer   GVP - Group vice president
COO - Chief operating officer   GC - Group controller
CFO - Chief financial officer   DGM - Division general manager
  CC - Corporate controller   DC - Division controller

Top management: CEO and those reporting directly to that position
Division management: DGM and those reporting directly to that position

Depending on the scope of responsibilities assumed by the chief executive officer, there may or may not be a separate chief operating officer position. Where a separation of responsibilities exists, the chief operating officer is the one most actively involved in the day-to-day running of the business. If the corporation has more than 15 or 20 divisions, there frequently is a position of group vice president in between the chief executive officer and the chief operating officer and the division general manager, with 4 to 5 divisions reporting to each group vice president. If the group vice president position exists, there may or may not be staff executives—including a group controller—reporting to the group vice president, depending on the scope of the group vice president's responsibilities.

The term "division" is used loosely to refer to branches, departments, subsidiaries—virtually any organizational unit. Here it is used to refer to a *business unit* concerned with the development, manufacture, and sale of a range of related product lines, for example, commercial refrigeration equipment or industrial chemicals. The division general manager typically is a "mini-CEO" responsible for all aspects of the division's business—finance, engineering, manufacturing, sales, and so on. The scope of these functions at the division level may vary depending on the degree to which they are centralized at corporate headquarters.

In the case of the finance function, there is typically no position at the division level equivalent to that of the chief financial officer at the corporate level. This is because financial responsibilities other than controllership are usually centralized. The division controller is the top financial executive in the division and typically reports directly to the division general manager with a functional or "dotted line" responsibility to the corporate controller. To the extent that the data processing function is centralized or separated from the controllership function, the extent of the division controller's responsibility for this function diminishes. Regardless of how the long-range planning function is organized at corporate headquarters, the division controller is typically responsible for this activity because there is usually no separate planning function at the division level.

Divisions with manufacturing plants typically have plant controllers who report directly to the manufacturing plant manager with functional or "dotted line" responsibility to the division controllers. Less frequently, there may be controllers in other functional departments within the division—such as marketing controllers or purchasing controllers—who also report on a "dotted line" to the division controller.

Focus of the Study

In this study, the focus is on the corporate controllers and the division controllers only. Controllers at other organizational levels, for example, group controllers or controllers in manufacturing, marketing, or purchasing departments, are not considered. Further, from among the multitude of factors relevant to an understanding of controller involvement at these levels, the influence of a limited set is investigated—characteristics of the company's environment, business, and management. No attempt is made to investigate the influence of the controller's motivation or personability, the quality of the controller's interpersonal relationships with mangement, or other characteristics of the particular individual occupying the controller position studied. These and other factors are important, as described in the introduction in Part II, but they are not studied so as to keep the project manageable. The broad research question asked is, "Quite apart from the effects of motivation, personality, interpersonal relationships, and other characteristics associated with the particular individual serving as controller, what is the influence of the company's environment, business, and management on the degree of controller involvement?"

CONCEPTUAL FRAMEWORK

Once the organization arena for this study is defined as the corporate and division levels of large, multidivisional companies, it is possible to build on prior research in these settings. However, since this prior work does not deal with controller involvement in business decisions, it does not directly yield hypotheses for the study. Rather, it suggests major concepts that may be important, and these concepts are used to direct the investigation. In subsequent chapters specific hypotheses are developed and examined with data. This chapter merely introduces the basic conceptual framework and briefly outlines how the major concepts drawn from the prior research and other variables in three major areas—the company's environment, business, and management—are relevant to the present study (Exhibit 3-2).

An important characteristic of the company's operating environment that affects management's demand for information, and hence controller involvement, is its rate of change.[1] In an environment characterized by rapidly changing products and markets, for instance, management is likely to place great emphasis on quick decision making, requiring the controller to provide timely information and analyses as rapidly as needed. Such a role for the controller, calling for increased involvement in decision making, may be far less important for a company operating in a more stable product market environment.

Another characteristic of the company's environment that may have an important influence on the controller involvement is its operating interdependence.[2] One stream of research that suggests the importance of this concept for the present study is from the field of organizational behavior. This work indicates that interdependence has an important influence on the organization's needs for coordination and control.[3] Since the controller may be involved in these management tasks, the controller's role may be influenced by the company's operating interdependence.

[1] Lawrence and Lorsch (1967); Galbraith (1973).

[2] Operating interdependence denotes the extent to which this company's product markets are interrelated. The greater the interrelatedness, the greater the operating interdependence.

[3] Thompson (1967); Lorsch and Allen (1973).

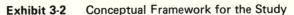

Exhibit 3-2   Conceptual Framework for the Study

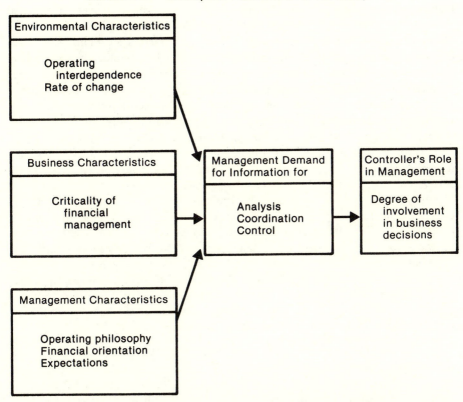

A related stream of research reinforcing the importance of this aspect of the operating environment for the controller's role is from business policy. Rumelt,[4] building on the work of Wrigley[5] and Berg,[6] proposes a scheme for broadly classifying large industrial organizations according to the diversification strategy—single business, dominant business, related business, and unrelated business. The scale represents decreasing levels of interrelatedness among the company's businesses. The greater the interrelatedness, the greater the potential benefit to be derived from closely coordinating the company's operations. To the extent that controllers are involved in such matters, for example, pricing intracompany sales, their role would be affected.

A characteristic of the company's business that could have an important influence on controller involvement is the extent to which sound financial management is *critical* to business success. In an era of continuing inflation and capital shortages, most companies recognize the importance of good financial management.

[4] Rumelt (1974).
[5] Wrigley (1970).
[6] Berg (1971).

However, for companies in certain types of businesses the importance of such management may be more critical than in others. For example, expense control and asset management may be more critical in businesses with low profit margins—such as meatpacking—than for a company where other factors are more critical—for example, research and development in the case of high-technology companies and marketing innovation in the case of cosmetics firms. Similarly, in a capital-intensive business, such as basic chemical manufacturing, sound financial analysis and investment may be more critical to the company's success than in less capital-intensive businesses. In companies for which financial management is more critical to success, the controller may play a more active role in business decision making.

Finally, management's operating philosophy, orientation, and expectations may have an important influence on controller involvement. Child,[7] Allen,[8] and Lorsch and Allen[9] discuss the critical role of operating philosophy in determining the company's management approach. To the extent that management chooses to emphasize analysis, coordination, and control of operations, the potential for controller involvement increases. Management's orientation can have a similar effect. To the extent that management is financially oriented—seeks financial information in running the business—the opportunity for controller involvement increases. Management's expectations regarding the controller's role can also influence controller involvement. As the literature on "role theory" indicates, behavior in a given role is influenced by the expectations of those in the person's "role set," that is, those with whom the person must deal in performing the role.[10]

METHODOLOGY

The research design and data collection were carefully planned to permit an examination of concepts from earlier work for their possible relevance to the subject under investigation. The study can thus be linked to earlier work with different emphasis but in the same organizational arena, that is, corporate and division levels of large, multidivisional industrial companies.

Whenever possible, variables and concepts from this earlier work were used in this investigation. Details concerning the measurement of these variables, and their sources, are included in the Methodological Appendix. As the investigation proceeded, other dimensions of importance emerged. Systematic measurements could be developed for some of these and are also included in the appendix. It was not possible to develop such measurements in other cases, so some of the data presented are qualitative, for example, interview quotations.

[7] Child (1972).

[8] Allen (1978).

[9] Lorsch and Allen (1973).

[10] Katz and Kahn (1978). This is the approach taken by Hopper (1978) in the study of 12 management accountants cited in Chapter 1.

Research Phases

A summary of the various research phases is shown in Exhibit 3-3. Each of these phases is now described.

Preliminary field work was conducted in four companies prior to undertaking this study. The purpose of these initial visits was to get acquainted with the research territory in preparation for a more intensive investigation. These data are not presented here.

Phase 1 of the study began in the summer of 1977 with visits to five companies that agreed to participate on the basis of prior contact with the researcher or his faculty colleagues. From earlier contacts it appeared that the companies differed in terms of the overall level of controller involvement—three seemed to have "strong" controllers, the other two less so. It was felt that a great deal could be learned by comparing and contrasting these companies.

The typical interview schedule followed when visiting companies is shown in Exhibit 3-4. The following executives were interviewed at corporate headquarters: the chief executive officer, the chief financial officer, the corporate controller, the head of internal audit, the executive working closely with the financial control system, and the personnel executive most familiar with the company's controllers. Two or three typical divisions of each company were also visited and the following executives interviewed in each: the division general manager, one operating executive reporting to the division general manager, the division controller, and one person reporting to the division controller. The corporate controller and the corporate personnel executive were interviewed for two hours each; all others for one hour each.

Most interviews were unstructured. However, structured interviews and questionnaires—based on previous research and the preliminary field work—were also used on a limited basis. The experience and learning from this phase of the study led to the formulation of additional questionnaires to facilitate subsequent field work. The personal insights and observations gained from this and some earlier work are reported in two publications for practitioners prepared by the author.[11]

Phase 2 of the study was more systematic and extensive. It would have been preferable to have examined companies that could be compared and contrasted directly on variables in the conceptual framework and other dimensions that were emerging as important. However, given the nature of the variables (Exhibit 3-2), such information was not readily available and the procedure was infeasible. Instead, companies were selected from the *Forbes* "30th Annual Report on American Industry"[12] using two criteria to be mentioned shortly. The following basic industry categories were chosen: chemicals, conglomerates, construction and building equipment, energy, foods, forest products and packaging, health care products, industrial equipment, information processing, and metals. In each subcategory of all

---

[11] Sathe (1978a; 1978b).

[12] "30th Annual Report on American Industry," *Forbes*, January 9, 1978.

Exhibit 3-3 Research Phases

Research Phase	Year	Number of Companies	Purpose	Data Collection	Data Included in the Study?
Preliminary	1976	4	Initial orientation to the research territory	Unstructured field interviews	No
1	1977	5	Comparison and contrast of companies with different levels of controller involvement	Unstructured and structured field interviews; limited questionnaires	Yes
2	1978	19[a]	Comparison and contrast of companies differing in financial performance and industry classification	Unstructured and structured field interviews; several questionnaires	Yes

[a]The chief executive officers of 208 companies were contacted for participation, 134 (64 percent) responded, and 23 (11 percent) agreed to participate. Of these, 19 could be included within the time available for the study. Three of these requested that participants be given the option of not completing the questionnaires. As such, the quantitative data in these 3 companies are spotty.

Exhibit 3-4   List of Executives Typically Interviewed in Each Company

Corporate headquarters
    Chief executive officer or alternate (top operating executive)
    Chief financial officer or equivalent
    Corporate controller (two hours)
    Head of internal audit
    Executive working most closely with the financial control system
    Personnel executive most familiar with the company's controllers (two hours)

Division A
    Division general manager or alternate (top operating executive)
    One other senior operating executive
    Division controller
    One person reporting to the division controller

Division B
    Same list as shown for Division A

Details regarding typical interview schedule
    Unless indicated otherwise, all interviews were one hour in duration.

To the extent possible, the interviews were scheduled as follows: corporate controller (one hour, orientation), head of internal audit, financial control system executive, personnel executive, Division A, Division B, corporate controller (one hour, concluding interview), chief financial officer, chief executive officer.

The objective in arranging such a sequence of interviews was to get an initial overview from corporate staff executives before digging into a couple of typical divisions to study the operations more closely. The senior-most executives were interviewed toward the end to obtain their views on issues emerging from the researcher's understanding of the company's situation.

---

these basic industry categories, the chief executives of the 8 companies with the best and the 8 companies with the worst financial performance (five-year average of return on equity) were contacted for participation. Where an industry category in the *Forbes* listing had less than 16 companies, all the companies listed in the category were contacted. In all, 208 companies were contacted, 134 (64 percent) responded, 23 (11 percent) agreed to participate, and 19 (9 percent) could be visited within the time available for this study.

The extensive interviewing required (14 interviews totaling 16 hours of interview time at the senior-most levels in each company) considerably dampened the response rate. This was the reason most frequently cited (37 percent) by those declining to participate.[13] No attempt was made to determine what the non-

---

[13] Other reasons commonly given when declining participation were company reorganization (14 percent) and company policy (8 percent). Twenty-four percent of the respondents did not indicate why they would not participate.

response bias might be. Nor did the selection procedure represent statistical random sampling. Rather, industries and companies were contacted on the basis of two criteria.

First, high and low financial performers were sought to permit examination of the relationship between controller involvement and company financial performance. Second, industry categories were picked to offer sufficient variation in terms of operating interdependence. For example, the forest products companies were integrated vertically and were characterized by high interdependence. On the other hand, most of the conglomerates were in unrelated businesses and were characterized by low interdependence. The presence of such variation in the companies studied would, it was hoped, facilitate the development and examination of hypotheses based on the conceptual framework.

Phase 2 of the study was undertaken during 1978. Questionnaires as well as structured and unstructured interviews were used. Questionnaires varied somewhat depending on the organizational position of the respondent. Those at corporate headquarters were asked more questions about the company as a whole; divisional executives were asked more questions about their particular division. Managers were asked to provide their impressions of their controller's role as well as their opinion of how this contributed to the running of the business. Controllers were asked these questions as well as others tailored to their particular perspectives. An appropriate questionnaire was mailed to each participant in advance of the visit with a request that it be completed and held until the interview. The first part of the interview was devoted to a discussion of the participant's questionnaire responses followed by structured and unstructured questions. Details are included in the Methodological Appendix.

Data Collection and Data Analysis

It must be emphasized that the questionnaires were used to *facilitate* data collection in sufficient depth and breadth within the interview time available. They were not viewed as "validated instruments" or used as substitutes for the interviews. When questionnaires were reviewed with the respondents with questions such as "What did you have in mind when you circled this response?" or "Can you give me an illustration of this?," there were occasionally some "gaps" between the questionnaire responses and what was actually revealed in the personal conversations. Only those questionnaires found to yield meaningful data were used in the analysis. Thus, validation of the questionnaires is based on the researcher's experience with them in the field rather than on statistical methodology. Measurements of other variables are based on questions asked during the interviews and are open to the usual criticisms concerning interviewer bias and scaling error. *In general, however, the questionnaire and interview measurements are considered to be valid rough assessments and sufficiently robust for an exploratory data analysis.*

Companies visited during the preliminary field work were excluded from the analysis. Only those visited in phases 1 and 2 were included. In the former, few executives, mostly controllers, were interviewed. Given the lack of balance and depth, there was not sufficient confidence in the data. In the latter, the variety and number of executives interviewed (see Exhibit 3-4) gave reasonable assurance about the validity of the data.

While structured interviews and questionnaires were used throughout the study, the primary role of the researcher was that of a "detective." If, during the data collection, there was any conflict between pursuing an unexpected but intriguing lead and following the structured interview and questionnaire schedule, the *former* was chosen. A practice followed to draw out potential informants was to keep mealtime open on the interview schedule. If a person seemed willing to divulge important or sensitive information, the interview was continued over lunch or dinner. Such conversations, away from the formality and limitations of the office, sometimes yielded valuable material for the study.

The interviewing strategy offered the flexibility necessary for an adventurous exploration of the research territory. The cost, however, was that qualitative or quantitative data on identical topics were not obtained in *all* companies. Nevertheless, because a fairly large number of companies was studied, each of the relationships inferred is based on several observations.

The inferred relationships emerged from an analysis of each company's situation and from repeated comparisons of similar and different situations. The procedure followed was to study all available data on one company—annual reports and other background information, interview notes, and questionnaire data—for half a day or more and then to prepare a brief (10- to 15-page) written analysis of the situation. Causal diagrams were drawn when possible to indicate how various factors appeared to be influencing others. The procedure was repeated for each company.

Next, companies were grouped according to common "patterns" or "syndromes" in an attempt to discover higher-order generalizations. Thus, all companies in which controllers appeared to be actively involved in business decisions were studied as a group to see which similarities helped to explain the high level of controller involvement. Conversely, the common themes in the companies with a low level of controller involvement were also examined.

The generalizations derived from this qualitative analysis were stated as hypotheses and were *examined* with the available quantitative data. The procedure used does not constitute hypothesis *testing* because the hypotheses were inferred from all available information, including the quantitative data. The phrase "hypotheses examination" is used simply to denote the obtaining of a statistical association for the hypotheses generated via the process of qualitative analysis described in the two preceding paragraphs. This use of statistical data is in the spirit of what has been referred to as *exploratory data analysis*[14] and should be clearly distinguished from its common use in the confirmatory data analysis of hypotheses testing.

The generated hypotheses related an "independent" variable—an aspect of the environment, business, or management—to a "dependent" variable—the degree of

[14] Tuckey (1977).

controller involvement. Examination of these hypotheses using simple correlational analysis revealed the strength of association between the dependent variable and each independent variable considered separately. Auxilliary hypotheses were examined to a limited extent to explore how other factors were associated with those independent variables that were found to be related to the dependent variable. More complicated analysis of the interrelationships between various factors and their effects on the dependnt variable was not undertaken. Although statistical multivariate techniques can be employed for such an examination, their meaningful use requires data on more cases than were available.[15]

Measurement of the variables is based on one of three sources of data: documents, interviews, or questionnaires. Variable numbers are prefixed by the letter "D", "I", or "Q" to indicate the data source. For example, the variable for company financial performance relative to the industry is labled "D1" to indicate that this variable was computed from documents (company and industry financial reports). Details concerning the measurement of all variables used in the statistical analysis are included in the Methodological Appendix at the end of the book.

Certain methodological issues concerning variable measurement and the statistical associations obtained therefrom may be noted. Since the dependent variables—controller involvement in a division (Q5), at corporate headquarters (Q6), and in the typical company division (Q7)—are all measured via questionnaires, their statistical associations with those contextual variables also measured via questionnaires are subject to method bias,[16] that is, may be distorted because of errors associated with a common measurement method. This is why it was decided to prefix the variable designations (with the letters "D", "I", or "Q") so the reader is alerted to this potential problem where it occurs.

To address the method bias problem, an attempt was made to obtain measurements of the dependent and contextual variables via different methods of measurement whenever possible. Since the former are all tapped using questionnaires, the method bias problem does not arise where the contextual variables are measured via either documents or interviews. For contextual variables measured via questionnaires, an attempt was made to limit the problem by using a different set of respondents in computing the dependent variables (refer to the Methodological Appendix for details).

How should the individual responses be combined in such computations? Some researchers have weighted individual scores according to their social position.[17] However, such a procedure must deal with several complex questions concerning selection of positions, their relative weighting to reflect differential importance, and the treatment of members with multiple roles. The procedure more commonly used

---

[15] For multivariate correlational analysis, Nunnally (1967, p. 164) recommends between five and ten times as many observations as there are variables. Similar ratios are typically recommended for path analysis and/or simultaneous estimation models (Blalock, 1964).

[16] Campbell and Fiske (1959).

[17] Hage and Aiken (1967).

is to assign equal weight to the score of each individual and to compute a simple average value.[18] This is the procedure followed in this study.

Presentation and Discussion of Results

The following format is used for presenting and discussing the results in Part II: the generated hypothesis is stated, the underlying rationale is developed, and the results are presented. Qualitative data, including quotations from the interview notes, are sometimes provided as illustrative material, and coefficients of correlation and other quantitative measures are used as appropriate to examine the stated hypothesis.

Although results of statistical tests of signifiance are presented for the statistical associations obtained with the quantitative data, this represents their use as a *classificatory device,* as presently explained, and should not be confused with their normal use for drawing generalizations about the population from which the observed sample was drawn. A statistical random sample of companies was not studied, as was mentioned previously, and it is not suggested that these results are representative of any particular population of companies. In fact, because the study is concerned with generation of hypotheses rather than with hypotheses testing, the application of statistical inference techniques is neither necessary nor very helpful, as Glaser and Strauss point out:

> Statistical tests of significance of an association between variables are not necessary when the discovered associations between indices are used for suggesting hypotheses. . . .
>
> These tests direct attention away from theoretically interesting relationships that are not of sufficient magnitude to be statistically significant. . . .
>
> Believing in tests of significance can also dissuade one from trusting consistent but weak relationships within and between consistency indices. Yet consistency validates the merit of relationships when it comes to the plausible reasoning required in a credible theoretical analysis.[19]

It was possible to examine some of the hypotheses generated with multiple sets of data, that is, for corporate controller involvement, division controller involvement, and typical division controller involvement. "Consistency validation" of other hypotheses remains the province of future research.

The generated hypotheses are used to construct descriptive "models" indicating the magnitude of the statistical association between various contextual factors and the degree of controller involvement, and it is in this connection that the statistical tests of significance have been used. The magnitude of the statistical association is classified as "strong" if the results would have been judged statisti-

---

[18] Lynch (1974).
[19] Glaser and Strauss (1967), pp. 200-201.

cally significant[20] below the .01 level under classical hypothesis testing; "moderate" for p values between .10 and .01, and "weak" for p values between .20 and .10. The magnitude of the association is considered "negligible" for p values greater than .20.

What is being sought is a procedure for classifying the various hypotheses according to the strength of the statistical association between the variables. A classification scheme based on the actual magnitude of the correlation between the variables (e.g., "A correlation greater than 0.50 indicates a "strong" association) or some other chosen index of the strength of the relationship between the variables could just as well have been employed. However, since researchers are accustomed to interpreting statistical results with the aid of tests of significance, these tests were chosen as the basis for *classifying the hypotheses* according to the magnitude of the statistical association between the variables. To repeat, such use should not be confused with the usual application of statistical tests of significance for drawing generalizations about the representative population.

Based on this classification of hypotheses, descriptive models are developed linking the contextual factors (that is, characteristics of the company's environment, business, and management) to the degree of controller involvement. A "strong" association is indicated by linking the appropriate variables with a *double solid* line in the descriptive models. If the association is "moderate," the variables are connected with a *solid* line, and a "weak" association is represented by a *dashed* line. Hypotheses with "negligible" statistical associations are *not represented* in the descriptive models of controller involvement to be developed.

Background information on the 24 companies for which data are analyzed and presented (companies in phase 1 and phase 2) is summarized in Exhibit 3-5. The company identification numbers shown are used when referring to these companies in the book.

Exhibit 3-5   Background Information on Companies

Company Identification Number	Industry Category[a]	Company Financial Performance Relative to Average of its Industry Category[b] (1 = low, 5 = high)	Operating Interdependence[c] (1 = low, 3 = high)
1	Metals	1	2
2	Foods	2	2
3	Energy	1	3
4	Energy	4	3
5	Forest products and packaging	4	3
6	Health care	3	1

[20] The word "significance" in this context does *not* refer to the importance of the finding. The .10 level of statistical significance ($p = .10$) represents a 10 percent probability of error in rejecting the null hypothesis, the .20 level a 20 percent probability of error.

Exhibit 3-5 (continued)

Company Identification Number	Industry Category[a]	Company Financial Performance Relative to Average of its Industry Category[b] (1 = low, 5 = high)	Operating Interdendence[c] (1 = low, 3 = high)
7	Construction	2	1
8	Forest products and packaging	2	2
9	Conglomerate	3	1
10	Building equipment	4	2
11	Chemicals	1	3
12	Industrial equipment	3	2
13	Energy	4	3
14	Foods	5	2
15	Foods	3	2
16	Conglomerate	5	1
17	Foods	2	3
18	Chemicals	5	3
19	Information processing	4	2
20	Information processing	2	3
21	Conglomerate	5	1
22	Building equipment	1	2
23	Conglomerate	5	2
24	Construction	5	1

[a]Based on classification used in *Forbes'* "30th Annual Directory of American Industry."

[b]Based on five-year financial performance *relative to its industry category* (variable D1 in the Methodological Appendix).

[c]Based on degree of intracompany transfers of products and services (variable D3 in the Methodological Appendix).

The next three chapters contain the development of the specific hypotheses, their examination with statistical data, and the building of descriptive models of controller involvement. The first of these, Chapter 4, focuses on the degree of involvement of the corporate controller at headquarters. Subsequent chapters deal with the degree of involvement of a division controller and the degree of *typical* division controller involvement in the company.

chapter 4

Degree of Corporate Controller Involvement at Headquarters

This chapter begins with an examination of how variables in the conceptual framework (Exhibit 3-2) and other contextual factors are related to the degree of corporate controller involvement at headquarters. Six specific hypotheses are developed, each relating one contextual variable to the degree of controller involvement. An examination of these hypotheses with the available quantitative data permits the development of a descriptive model linking contextual variables to the degree of controller involvement. The various hypotheses developed are used in the next chapter when considering the analogous phenomena within a division of the company.[1]

Three other sets of hypotheses are then developed and examined. The first set explores the question of how various factors, including management's emphasis on controller independence, are related to management's expectations regarding controller involvement. The second set examines the reasons for management's varying emphasis on controller indepedence. The last set of hypotheses relates certain corporate controller characteristics to the degree of corporate controller involvement.

CONTEXTUAL FACTORS AND CONTROLLER INVOLVEMENT

The six hypotheses developed in this section are summarized in Exhibit 4-1 along with the statistical data used to examine them. What follows is an elaboration of the rationale underlying these hypotheses and the supporting evidence.

---

[1] Data to be presented in this chapter and subsequent ones will be identified by variable numbers in parentheses following the variable name. Details concerning the measurement of these variables are included in the Methodological Appendix.

Rate of Change of Corporate Business Environment

Hypothesis 4-1
The greater the rate of change of the corporate business environment, the higher the degree of corporate controller involvement in business decisions.

The controller can be of great assistance to management by performing appropriate analysis and special studies as required. This is especially important in a company facing an unstable environment, where the need for quick decisions and rapid response are particularly great. Under these circumstances, relevant, reliable, and timely information and analysis would appear to be crucial to success. Since the corporate controller has an opportunity to contribute in this area, the degree of controller involvement should be directly influenced by the rate of change of corporate business environment. When examined with the quantitative data, however, the statistical association is in a direction opposite to that predicted by the hypothesis (see Exhibit 4-1). To repeat, the hypothesis was generated from a *qualitative* analysis of all the data (see Chapter 3, Data Collection and Data Analysis).

Degree of Operating Interdependence

Hypothesis 4-2
The greater the operating interdependence, the higher the degree of corporate controller involvement in business decisions.

As several authors point out, the controllership function performs an integration role in organizations.[2] For example, one of the most important objectives of budgeting—a controllership activity—is the achievement of coordination among the company's operations. The controller also assists in the achievement of overall coordination via pricing of intracompany transfers of goods and services. Since the potential benefit from closely coordinating company activities increases with increasing operating interdependence,[3] the potential for controller involvement also increases.

When examined with the quantitative data the magnitude of the statistical association is weak (Exhibit 4-1). This hypothesis may be reexamined using a scheme from the business policy literature that classifies companies according to diversification strategy: single business, dominant business, related business, and unrelated business.[4] The criterion of "degree of relatedness among the company's businesses" used in this scheme represents varying degrees of operating interdependence within the company.

[2] Heckert and Willson (1967); Horngren (1967); Lorsch and Allen (1973).
[3] Lorsch and Allen (1973).
[4] Wrigley (1970); Rumelt (1974).

Exhibit 4-1 Examination of Hypotheses Relating Contextual Variables and Corporate Controller Involvement (Q6)[a]

Hypothesis Number	Contextual Variables	Hypothesized Direction of Association between Contextual Variable and Controller Involvement	Coefficient of Correlation or Other Statistical Evidence	Number of Observations	Magnitude of the Statistical Association[b]
4-1	Rate of change of corporate business environment				
	Overall rate of change (Q9)	+	−.08	14	Negligible
	Number of aspects of corporate business environment subject to rapid change (Q10)	+	−.21	14	Negligible
	Composite index of rate of corporate environmental change (Q11)	+	−.16	14	Negligible
4-2	Company operating interdependence (D3)	+	0.34*	21	Weak
4-3	Criticality of financial analysis and control				
	Capital asset intensity (D6)	+	0.29*	21	Weak
	Working asset intensity (D7)	+	−0.14	21	Negligible

Exhibit 4-1 (continued)

Hypothesis Number	Contextual Variables	Hypothesized Direction of Association between Contextual Variable and Controller Involvement	Coefficient of Correlation of Other Statistical Evidence	Number of Observations	Magnitude of the Statistical Association[b]
	Operating margin (D8)	–	–0.01	20	Negligible
4-4	Corporate management's financial ability				
	CEO has financial background (D4)	–	In Exhibit 4-4*		Weak
	Percentage of senior corporate executives with financial background (D5)	–	–0.32*	20	Weak
4-5	Corporate management's financial orientation (I8)	+	In Exhibit 4-6**		Moderate
4-6	Corporate management's expectations regarding corporate controller involvement (Q2)	+	0.70***	15	Strong

[a] Numbers in parentheses refer to variable numbers in the Methodological Appendix.

[b] See Chapter 3, Presentation and Discussion of Results. Had the observations been a statistical random sample (which they were not), the p values would be as follows: * $p < .20$, ** $p < .10$, *** $p < .01$.

Exhibit 4-2 Degree of Corporate Controller Involvement Under Various Diversification Strategies[a,b,c]

	Average Degree of Corporate Controller Involvement for				
				Unrelated Business	
Company	Single Business	Dominant Business	Related Business	Passive	Acquisitive[d]
Number of companies in each category	1	5[e]	8	6	4[f]
Average score on the degree of corporate controller involvement (Q6)	18.0	13.8	14.4	12.0	10.0

[a] Classification of diversification strategies is from Rumelt (1974).

[b] Numbers in parentheses refer to variables in the Methodological Appendix.

[c] Had the observations been a statistical random sample (which they were not), the differences between groups would be statistically significant below the .10 level ($F_{3,17} = 2.982$). (Since the single business category has only one observation, it was folded into the dominant business group in computing the F value.)

[d] Commonly referred to as "conglomerates."

[e] Data on two of these companies were unavailable.

[f] Data on one of these companies were unavailable.

Data on degree of controller involvement classified by company diversification strategy are summarized in Exhibit 4-2. These data indicate that the degree of controller involvement in the "unrelated business" category is on the average lower than in the other three categories. Further, the "acquisitive" category—companies that have diversified rapidly by means of mergers and acquisitions (the "conglomerates")—appear to have the lowest degrees of corporate controller involvement. This is probably due to the fact that the administrative structure in these firms tends to be quite "lean" at the top and concerned primarily with the allocation of capital among its portfolio of businesses.[5] In this setting, the treasurership aspects of financial management, particularly investor relations and capital financing, are probably more important than controllership. (Refer to Exhibit 1-1 for a review of the distinction between treasurership and controllership.) As the corporate controller in company 18 explained, "In a conglomerate firm there is heavy reliance on finance, but the emphasis is primarily on portfolio management. In a highly integrated firm such as ours, the role of finance is more complicated because of the product integration and the high degree of product transfers across divisional lines."

[5] Berg (1971).

Importance of Financial Analysis and Control

Hypothesis 4-3

The greater the importance of financial analysis and financial control to business success, the higher the degree of corporate controller involvement in business decisions.

Since the current economic climate is characterized by inflation and capital shortages, all companies pay attention to financial analysis and financial control.[6] However, depending on the nature of the business, in some companies such analysis and control are particularly critical. Examples are capital-asset-intensive[7] companies in which sound financial analysis is valued given the special role of capital investment decisions, working-asset-intensive[8] companies in which management of inventories and receivables is particularly important, and low-operating-margin[9] businesses in which cost control is vital. Where such issues and decisions are critical to business success, the degree of controller involvement is likely to be greater than in other cases because the controller provides information and analysis bearing on these issues and related decisions.

The following financial indicators are used as surrogates for the underlying dimension "importance of financial analysis and control": capital asset intensity, working asset intensity, and operating margin. Higher capital asset intensity and working asset intensity or lower margins are considered indicative of greater importance of financial analysis and control. The correlations between these variables and degree of controller involvement are shown in Exhibit 4-1. The association is weak for capital asset intensity and negligible for the other two indicators.

To summarize the results presented so far, operating interdependence and capital

---

[6] The essence of "control" is action that adjusts operations to achieve predetermined objectives (Sherwin, 1956). Such action is based on information that management obtains from various sources: visual inspection, phone conversations, reading reports, and so on. "Financial control" refers to control based on financial data (Lawler and Rhode, 1976). A survey of 149 manufacturing companies undertaken in 1965 found that four areas of business activity are most susceptible to financial control: operating costs and expenses, capital expenditures, inventories, and receivables (Harkins and Thompson, 1965).

[7] Capital asset intensity is defined as fixed assets divided by net sales. The work of Bower (1970) indicates that traditional capital budgeting theory is inadequate for explaining how capital investment decisions are actually made. Financial analysis is only one of several important inputs contributing to the decision-making process, of course.

[8] Working asset intensity is defined as inventories plus receivables divided by net sales.

[9] Operating margin equals operating income (net sales less operating expenses) divided by net sales.

intensity are the two contextual variables with a more than negligible statistical association with the degree of controller involvement. Since both these associations are weak, they are represented by dashed lines in the partial "model" of corporate controller involvement shown in Exhibit 4-3. This descriptive model is developed further as the discussion proceeds and the effects of other variables on controller involvement are examined.

Management's Financial Ability

Hypothesis 4-4
The greater the degree of management's financial ability, the lower the degree of corporate controller involvement.

This hypothesis may appear to be counterintuitive, but there are two conflicting forces at work. On the one hand, a financially trained corporate management may provide additional status and an opportunity for greater involvement for the corporate controller. On the other hand, the opportunity for controller involvement may be less when the chief executive officer and/or a larger number of senior corporate executives have financial backgrounds because, even if these executives encourage becoming actively involved, the controller may find it difficult to do so. The essence of active involvement is the ability to recommend courses of action and challenge the analysis and plans of operating executives. This is not easily done

Exhibit 4-3   Summary of Relationships Between Environmental and Business Characteristics and Corporate Controller Involvement

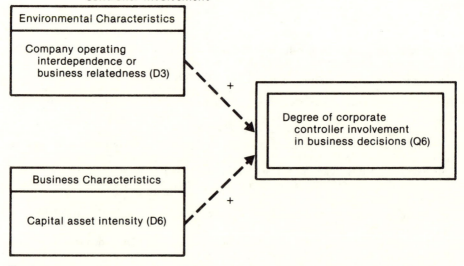

Numbers in parentheses refer to variables in the Methodological Appendix. Dashed lines indicate a weak statistical association.

under normal conditions and probably becomes more difficult when one's superior and colleagues are experts in one's area of potential contribution.

Two indicators of management's financial ability are used to examine this hypothesis: whether or not the chief executive officer has a financial background and the percentage of senior corporate executives with financial backgrounds. For both indicators the magnitude of the statistical association is weak (see Exhibit 4-1). Chief executive officers with financial backgrounds as well as larger numbers of corporate executives having financial training restrict the degree of corporate controller involvement.

To illustrate the relationships, consider the following interview quotations from company 6, in which the chief executive officer had been the company's corporate controller. According to the chief executive officer, "My background within the company has been in the controllership area. Hence, I take considerable interest in financial aspects and have considerable influence in financial matters. I have less influence in marketing, because of my own background and abilities." According to the chief financial officer, "The CEO is an incredible analyst. He does a detailed analytical job." According to the corporate controller, "Our CEO is a finance man. He is deeply involved and knowledgeable in the finance area." The corporate controller involvement is "dampened" on account of the financial ability of the chief executive officer because the chief executive officer in effect serves as his or her own controller. The same phenomenon helps to explain why the presence of a large number of corporate executives with financial ability reduces controller involvement in decision making. As one corporate controller put it, "Magic is not mysterious to former magicians!"

Whether the "dampening effect" on controller involvement is associated primarily with the chief executive officer's financial background or with the larger percentage of senior executives having financial backgrounds, is not clear because the two indicators are themselves positively related as shown in Exhibit 4-4.

Exhibit 4-4   Management's Financial Ability and Degree of Corporate Controller Involvement[a]

CEO Has Financial Background (D4 = 2)			CEO Does not Have Financial Background (D4 = 1)		
Number of Companies	Average % of Senior Executives with Financial Backgrounds (D5)	Average Degree of Corporate Controller Involvement	Number of Companies	Average % of Senior Executives with Financial Backgrounds (D5)	Average Degree of Corporate Controller Involvement
7	39.3%[b]	10.8[c]	17	15.9%[b]	13.8[c]

[a]Numbers in parentheses refer to variables in the Methodological Appendix.

[b]Were the observations a statistical random sample (which they were not), the p value would be as follows: Difference in values when chief executive officer does and does not have financial background: $P < .01, t_{21} = 2.65$.

[c]Difference in values when chief executive officer does and does not have financial background: $P < .20, t_{19} = 1.32$.

In 7 of the 24 companies studied (29 percent),[10] the chief executive officer has a financial background.[11] In these companies, the percentage of senior corporate executives who also have financial backgrounds is much larger than in other companies. This suggests the possibility that there is a tendency toward "inbreeding" in organizations, that is, with executives appearing to surround themselves with persons of similar background.[12]

The associations between the two indicators of management's financial ability and controller involvement are shown by dashed lines in Exhibit 4-5 to indicate that they are weak. Further, the two "restricting variables" are themselves strongly and positively associated; that is, their independent effects on controller involvement are difficult to disentangle.

Management's Financial Ability
Versus Financial Orientation

A distinction is made between management's financial *ability* and financial *orientation* because this is useful in explaining varying degrees of controller involvement. These terms are first defined and a hypothesis is then developed relating this distinction to controller involvement.

Definitions

Financial orientation denotes the degree to which an executive relies on financial information and analysis and emphasizes financial control[13] in his or her approach to management.

Financial ability denotes the degree to which an executive is personally able to work with and interpret the significance of variances, trends, and other financial data and to use the financial control system effectively. Thus, an operating executive who came up through controllership would typically have a high degree of financial ability. But operating executives from other functional areas may possess similar ability by virtue of their skill and comfort level with numbers.

Executives with high financial ability understandably tend to be financially oriented. But, even if managers do not possess financial ability, they may still be

[10] One survey of 375 companies found that 23 percent of the chief executive officers had a predominantly financial background (Silverman, 1975).

[11] Defined in terms of professional qualifications, for example, a certified public accountant, or prior work experience in controllership. (Refer to variable D4 in the Methodological Appendix for details.)

[12] The work of Bowen (1971), which suggests the presence of a "personality type" in most organizations, is consistent with this finding.

[13] Definitions of the term "control" and "financial control" appear in footnote 6 of this chapter.

Exhibit 4-5   Summary of Relationships Concerning Management's Financial Ability and Degree of Corporate Controller Involvement

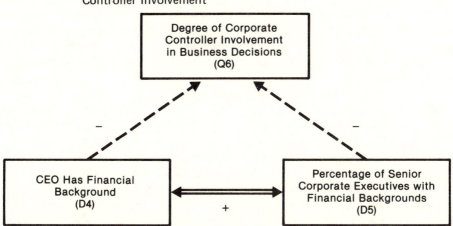

Numbers in parentheses refer to variables in the Methodological Appendix. Dashed lines indicate weak statistical associations. The double solid line indicates a strong statistical association.

financially oriented. This can occur in several ways as now described. At companies 8 and 19, management began to rely heavily on financial control after experiencing a severe profit decline. In the case of company 8 this occurred via a change in the top spot. The previous "hands-off" entrepreneurial chief executive officer was replaced by a "hands-on" financially oriented executive. At company 19, where profits plunged by 75 percent in 1975, the chief executive officer began to pay much more attention to financial control. According to him, "Following the tempo of rapid growth of the late sixties, we were extended as hell by 1973. We didn't have the right horses [balance sheet]. Then the collapse came in the fourth quarter of 1974. Inventories ballooned, receivables were out of hand, bank debt was out of sight, and profits disappeared.... We began to meet as a group [40 key people] to review three key asset management items monthly: inventories, receivables, and cost reductions. When we started this, it took us a long and agonizing three to six hours to complete the review because our managers didn't understand financial control techniques. Now it's down to one hour. If anyone thinks such changes can be made overnight, they are crazy. And it takes the dedication and active involvement of the chief executive officer to do it.... Historically, our receivables turned at 5 or 6 to 1. They got down to as low as 4 to 1 in 1975. We are now at 7.5 to 1. Our goal is 12 to 1."

Another cause of management's financial orientation lies in the nature of the company's business environment. According to the corporate controller at company 1, "During the last ten years, top management has become financially oriented because of our high costs and problems with the market."

Other causes for management's financial orientation may be traced to historical and personal factors. Company 14, for example, has had a long history of reliance on strong financial control, inculcated and institutionalized by the previous chief executive officer. The current generation of management continues to rely on strong financial controls. According to the company's chief operating officer, "The line executives in this company are financially oriented. I spend a lot of time with numbers. A few years back our assistant corporate controller attended Harvard's Advanced Management Program. What struck him was how little financial orientation other company operating executives had. This is not true here. There are historical reasons."

At company 23, top management placed heavy reliance on financial forecasts. This emphasis most likely resulted from the chief executive officer's particular style of management. According to the controller, "In this company, the financial measures of performance of operating units provide the keys to our way of managing. There is stong pressure for financial performance." According to the company's manager of financial forecasts, "At the review meetings, there is considerable peer pressure because numbers are being watched constantly. Forecasts provide a major focus." Said one company vice president (planning), "Financial forecasting is the single most important management tool." Said the chief financial officer, "Our chief executive officer is easy going and soft spoken. But he sets high financial performance standards."

Finally, management may be financially oriented because the controller has attempted and succeeded in "selling" operating executives on the virtues of financial control. Apparently this is a rather rare occurrence, if the companies studied are at all representative of large, industrial corporations. Only in the case of company 17 had the corporate controller taken upon himself the task of "educating" top management in financial control. According to this executive, who was highly regarded by the chief executive officer and by everyone else interviewed, "Our chief executive officer is a lawyer, with some background in personnel. In my opinion, he doesn't ask enough questions of a financial nature. . . . We have to educate the information users. It is a slow process. We must plant the financial seed, tend the seedling, and help the financial root system take hold. Once we get the operating people to upgrade their use of financial information, the whole company will benefit."

The distinction between financial ability and financial orientation has the following implications for controller involvement:

Hypothesis 4-5
The degree of corporate controller involvement is higher in companies where management is financially oriented, but does not have financial ability, than it is in other companies.

Management that is financially oriented by this definition is one that seeks financial information, analysis, and control in running the business. If such orientation derives from management's financial *ability*, however, the degree of corporate controller involvement is limited, as discussed under Hypothesis 4-4. Essentially, the opportunity for controller involvement arising out of management's financial orientation is then to some extent neutralized by its own financial ability. In effect, management supplies some of its own demand for financial information and analysis, acting partly as its own "controller."

On the other hand, if management's financial orientation stems from reasons other than financial ability, controller involvement could be high. Since management does not have the expertise to personally interpret and effectively use the financial information and analysis provided, the controller has the opportunity to make an important contribution.

Based on the data in Exhibit 4-6, the magnitude of the statistical association is moderate. The degree of corporate controller involvement is higher when management is financially oriented but without financial ability than it is in other cases.

Management's Expectations Regarding Controller Involvement

According to "role theory,"[14] the expectations of those with whom a person works in an organization have an important influence on the person's behavior. In the terminology and conceptual framework of role theory, the role being investigated is called the "focal role," and those with whom the person in the focal role must deal are called "role senders." The expectations of role senders are influenced by organizational factors and they in turn influence the behavior of the person in

Exhibit 4-6   Relationship of Management's Financial Ability, Financial Orientation, and Corporate Controller Involvement[a,b]

	Degree of Corporate Controller Involvement (Q6) When		
Company	Management Has Financial Ability (D4)	Management Has No Financial Ability but Is Financially Oriented (I8)	Management Neither Has Financial Ability nor Financial Orientation
Number of companies	7	8	6
Average degree of corporate controller involvement	12.0	16.8	10.2

[a] Numbers in parentheses refer to variables in the Methodological Appendix.

[b] Had the observations been a statistical random sample (which they are not), the differences between groups would be statistically significant below the .10 level ($F_{2,18} = 5.811$).

[14] Katz and Kahn (1978), Chap. 7

the focal role. These relationships are examined in this study with the controller in the focal role and management as the role senders.

Corporate management of the companies studied held very different expectations about the controller's role in decision making. A vivid illustration of this is provided by the following quotations from the interview notes. At company 6, the chief executive officer stated, "I expect a controller's role to be more creative than recording and analyzing data. He should be able to identify and isolate events in such a way that the corrective process will be easy. . . . If data are prepared by marketing, for example, the soundness and reasonableness of the underlying assumptions must be tested by the controller." The chief executive officer at company 10 described his expectations of the controller in these words: "The controllership function and its people are vital and key members of the management team at any level. The corporate controller is expected to be an equal and vital member in planning and be part of the corporate management team. Part of his job is to ask tough questions—hopefully motivational rather than hierarchical [political]." According to this company's chief financial officer, "The corporate controller's role is a balancing one, one of acting as the loyal opposition. He should play the role of devil's advocate. It is an art."

In contrast, the management at company 7 did not expect the controller to be actively involved. The following comments made by the company's financial executives indicate their dissatisfaction with the role as currently defined. According to the chief financial officer, "The corporate controller's role should be that of an activist. He should have an opinion on what the numbers ought to be. Very little effort has so far been devoted here toward that end." According to the company treasurer, "The coroporate controller's future role should go beyond number crunching." According to the newly recruited corporate controller, "At the _____ company, the corporate controller's role was much more of an activist type than it is here."

According to role theory, such varying expectations held by management (the role senders) should influence the corporate controller's role (the focal role).

Hypothesis 4-6

The higher the corporate management's expectations regarding the corporate controller's involvement in business decisions, the higher the degree of actual involvement.

When examined with quantitative data, the magnitude of the statistical association is strong (Exhibit 4-1). Since management's expectations are strongly related to the degree of actual involvement, possible reasons for management's varying expectations are explored in the next section of this chapter. A descriptive model of how various factors are related to the degree of corporate controller involvement

Exhibit 4-7   Contextual Factors and Corporate Controller Involvement

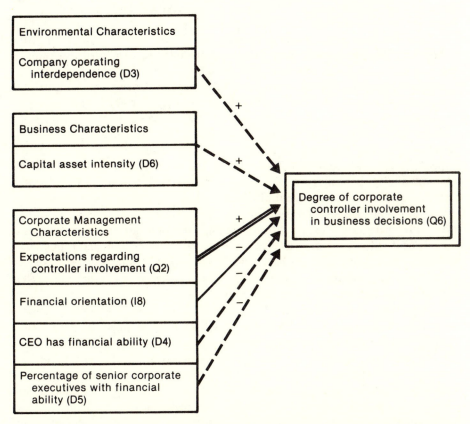

Numbers in parentheses refer to variables in the Methodological Appendix. Dashed lines represent weak statistical associations. The solid line indicates a moderate statistical association. The double solid line indicates a strong statistical association.

at headquarters, derived from an examination of the hypotheses in this section, is shown in Exhibit 4-7.

REASONS FOR MANAGEMENT'S VARYING EXPECTATIONS REGARDING CONTROLLER INVOLVEMENT

Although the reasons for management's varying expectations regarding the controller's role are difficult to identify, they seem ultimately to depend upon management's assumptions and beliefs about the best way to manage in a particular situation. These assumptions and beliefs may be influenced by prior education, training, and experience. To explore these possibilities, several hypotheses are examined.

As discussed in the supporting rationale for Hypotheses 4-1 through 4-5, the contextual variables in these hypotheses are predicted to be related to controller involvement because of increased opportunity for controller involvement under the conditions specified. For the same reasons, management may *expect* higher controller involvement under these conditions. Accordingly, five additional hypotheses are examined to discover the association between these contextual variables and management's expectations regarding controller involvement. The contextual variables are rate of change of corporate business environment, operating interdependence, importance of financial analyses and control, chief executive officer's financial ability, percentage of senior corporate executives with financial ability, and management's financial orientation.

As the results in Exhibit 4-8 show, working asset intensity has a strong association with management expectations regarding controller involvement, composite index of rate of environment change has a moderate association, and capital asset intensity and operating margin have a weak association with management expectations regarding controller involvement. The association of other contextual variables with management expectations is negligible.

Comparing these results with those obtained for the corresponding original hypotheses (4-1 and 4-3), higher capital asset intensity is associated with higher management expectations regarding controller involvement as well as higher actual involvement, although both relationships are weak. Higher working asset intensity, lower operating margin, and higher rate of change of corporate business environment, on the other hand, are associated with higher management expectations regarding controller involvement, but not with higher actual involvement. Thus, under these conditions, the "gap" between management expectations and actual involvement is wider than is otherwise the case.

One other factor that is related to management's varying expectations regarding controller involvement is management's emphasis on controller independence.

Hypothesis 4-6A
The greater the management emphasis on controller independence, the lower the management expectations regarding controller involvement.

As discussed in Chapter 1, the controller has the responsibility for financial reporting and custody of assets as well as the responsibility for contributing to business decisions. The former requires the maintenance of a degree of objectivity and independence; the latter requires active involvement. To the extent that these requirements are viewed as conflicting, an emphasis on one will be associated with a deemphasis of the other.

Exhibit 4-8 Relationships Among Contextual Variables and Management Expectations Regarding Corporate Controller Involvement in Business Decisions (Q2)[a]

Hypothesis Number	Contextual Variables	Hypothesized Direction of Association Between Contextual Variables and Management Expectations Regarding Controller Involvement	Correlation Coefficient	Number of Observations	Magnitude of the Statistical Association[b]
4-1A	Rate of change of corporate business environment				
	Overall rate of change	+	.16	15	Negligible
	Number of aspects of environment subject to rapid change (Q10)	+	.28	15	Negligible
	Composite index of rate of environment change (Q11)	+	.44**	15	Moderate
4-2A	Operating interdependence (D3)	+	−.13	16	Negligible
4-3A	Criticality of financial analysis and control				
	Capital asset intensity (D6)	+	.34*	16	Weak
	Working asset intensity (D7)	+	.69***	16	Strong
	Operating margin (D8)	−	−.41*	16	Weak
4-4A	Management's financial ability				
	CEO has financial background (D4)	+	.01	16	Negligible
	Percentage of senior corporate executives with financial background (D5)	+	−.22	16	Negligible
4-5A	Management's financial orientation (18)	+	.23	21	Negligible

[a]Numbers in parentheses refer to variable numbers in the Methodological Appendix.

[b]See Chapter 3, Presentation and Discussion of Results. Had the observations been a statistical random sample (which they were not), the p values would be as follows: $*p < .20$, $**p < .10$, $***p < .01$.

79

When examined with the quantitative data, the statistical association is of moderate magnitude.[15] Thus, management tends to view the controller's responsibility for financial reporting and internal control to be somewhat at odds with the responsibility for active involvement in business decisions. The following quotations from the interview notes illustrate how top management expectations regarding these controller responsibilities vary. According to the chief executive officer at company 6,

> Being an umpire is a role of a controller, but a secondary role. I consider accurate accounting, being impartial, and so on as important, but not as ends in themselves. I expect a controller's role to be more creative than recording and analyzing data. He should be able to identify and isolate events in such a way that the corrective process will be easy.

The chief executive officer at companies 2 and 5 placed greater emphasis on the reporting and monitoring role. According to the chief executive officer at company 2,

> I talk to the corporate controller if there is some question about an SEC requirement or an IRS regulation. Also if there is any concern about the accuracy of reporting or possible fraud. But the controller is not involved in business decisions. That is the province of line managers, not staff executives.

The chief executive officer at company 5 made the following comment:

> We believe that the corporate controller needs to have broad auditing experience. Public accounting offers that, and a more independent outlook than can be developed by someone who has been promoted from within the company. Compared to our competition, we have a fairly sophisticated accounting system and reasonably tight internal control. We get a good report card from our outside accountants and the government auditors who have reviewed our system on several occasions.

Possible reasons for management's varying expectations regarding controller independence are examined in the next section of this chapter. A schematic of how various contextual factors are related to management's expectations regarding controller involvement, derived from an examination of the hypotheses in this section, appears in Exhibit 4-9.

----

[15] The correlation between corporate management expectations regarding controller independence (variable Q22) and corporate management's expectation regarding controller involvement (Q2) is -0.46, based on 21 observations. Had these observations been a statistical random sample (which they were not), the results would be statistically significant below the .10 level.

Exhibit 4-9   Contextual Factors and Management's Expectations Regarding
Controller Involvement

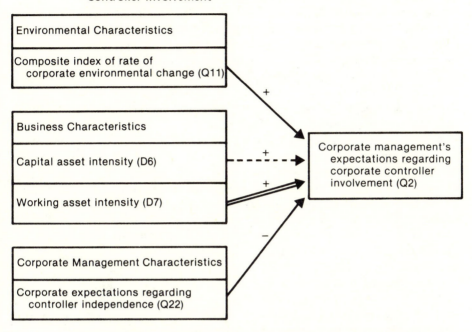

Numbers in parentheses refer to variables in the Methodological Appendix. Dashed line indicates a weak statistical association. Solid lines indicate moderate statistical associations. The double solid line indicates strong statistical association.

REASONS FOR MANAGEMENT'S VARYING EXPECTATIONS REGARDING CONTROLLER INDEPENDENCE

Concern About the Integrity of Financial Reporting and Internal Control

Hypothesis 4-A
The greater the management concern about the integrity of the company's financial reporting and/or the adequacy of its internal controls, the greater the management expectations regarding controller independence.

Since management is accountable to the stockholders, to the government, and to the regulatory agencies, management is well aware of the importance of accurate financial reporting and sound internal control. With the recent promulgation of the Foreign Corrupt Practices Act, for example, these matters are of particular concern. Such awareness and concern are acute if the company is subject to extreme public pressure and government regulation. The oil companies, for example, are required to comply with special rules and regulations concerning the accounting and reporting of petroleum production, inventory, and distribution. Management in these companies is also particularly sensitive about its public "image" following the oil embargo of 1973 and the subsequent public debate concerning whether or not the oil companies should be split up to increase competition and limit "excess profit." In these companies, management is extremely sensitive about any additional adverse publicity stemming from inaccurate reporting or control.

Even if management is not subject to such extreme pressure, it may nonetheless be particularly concerned about the integrity of the company's reporting and control system if it is experiencing, or has recently experienced, one or more of the following "surprises": (1) the discovery of fraud, defalcation, or illegal payments by company personnel; (2) "accounting surprises" or "blowups," for example, *unexpected* write-offs of inventory or receivables having significant adverse impact on corporate profit; and (3) *wide* and *frequent* discrepancies between projected and actual financial results.

Where management concern about the credibility of the financial reporting or internal control system is high, controller independence may be emphasized more than it is in other companies.

When examined with the quantitative data, the statistical association is of negligible magnitude.[16] However, it is noteworthy that the management of the three oil companies in the study (which were experiencing the greatest concern in this regard) all placed the highest emphasis on controller independence.

Environmental Stress

Hypothesis 4-B
The greater the degree of environmental stress, the higher the management expectations regarding controller independence.

As several studies have found,[17] management tends to tighten controls[18] when faced with a stressful situation. An example is the management emphasis on cost

---

[16] Based on 13 observations, the coefficient of correlation between management concern about the integrity of financial reporting and/or adequacy of internal control (variable I1) and management expectations regarding controller independence (variable Q22) is $-.09$. Had the observations been a statistical random sample (which they were not), this result would not be statistically significant below the .20 level.

[17] Herman (1963); Hall and Manfield (1971). Argyris (1953) and March and Simon (1958) also discuss this phenomenon.

[18] The "control process," broadly defined, is the process of setting organizational objectives, monitoring performance against these objectives, and taking corrective action toward the accomplishment of objectives. In the typical multidivisional company, monthly reviews of divisional financial performance against the budget are conducted by corporate executives as part of the control process, and the corporate controller typically administers the budget preparation and performance analysis system.

control and budget reduction when a company experiences a sharp decline in profits. Since valid information is particularly crucial when the company is experiencing financial stress, controller independence may be particularly emphasized under these conditions.

Based on the definition used in an earlier research study,[19] two related indicators of environmental stress are examined: declining profitability and low financial performance relative to the company's industry. The statistical associations for both indicators are of negligible magnitude.[20]

As was pointed out in the introduction to Part II, the primary focus in this part of the book is on examining the influence of contextual factors on controller involvement. The emphasis has been on understanding how characteristics of the situation, rather than of the particular individual occupying the controller's position, are related to the degree of controller involvement. The last section of this chapter considers the question of how three characteristics of the corporate controller—his or her allocation of time to various areas of responsibility, ability and motivation, and conflict resolution style—are related to the degree of involvement in business decisions.

CHARACTERISTICS OF THE CORPORATE CONTROLLER

Time Allocation to Areas of Responsibility

As has been mentioned, the controller has three major areas of responsibility: financial reporting, internal control, and contribution to business decisions. How the controller's allocation of time to these areas of responsibility influences involvement in business decisions is now examined.

Hypothesis 4-7
The greater the corporate controller's preoccupation with financial reporting and internal control, the lower the degree of involvement in business decisions.

Prior research (reviewed under Studies of Controller Involvement in Chapter 1) suggests that a major factor limiting the controller's involvement in decision making

---

[19] Following the terminology of the physical sciences, Hall and Mansfield (1971) conceptualized stress as "an external force operating on a system, be it an organization or a person" (p. 533). Environmental stress was then defined as "a marked decrease in available financial resources" (p. 535).

[20] Based on 18 observations, the coefficients of correlation between financial stress (variable D2)/financial performance (variable D1), and management expectations regarding controller independence (variable Q22) are $0.24/-.18$. Were the observations a statistical random sample (which they were not), the results would not be statistically significant below the .20 level. (Note: for variable D1, high stress is indicated by low financial performance; hence the negative correlation is in the right direction.)

is the financial reporting activity, which is clearly defined and programmed to a rigid schedule, thus taking up considerable time and attention. In contrast, the responsibility for contribution to the business decision-making process lacks formal specification and is therefore neglected. Although these previous studies do not examine the controller's responsibility for internal control, preoccupation with these activities may likewise limit the controller's involvement in business decisions. In general, as the preoccupation with other activities increases, the time and energy that the controller has available for participation in business decisions diminishes, thus limiting involvement.

Two sets of data are used to examine this hypothesis. The first set deals with the extent to which the controller's time is spent on meeting the demands of external agencies versus those of management. To the extent that the controller is preoccupied with the former, the time available for the latter is limited. When examined with the quantitative data, however, the statistical association is of negligible magnitude.[21]

The second set of data deals with the strength of the company's internal audit activity. Although most companies have a full-time corporate internal audit staff, the strength of the audit function varies from company to company. To the extent that the corporate internal audit activity is strong, the corporate controller has fewer concerns about internal control and more time for other responsibilities. Under these conditions, the degree of controller involvement in business decisions may be greater. When examined with the quantitative data, this association is of moderate magnitude.[22]

Thus, between the two major areas of the controller's responsibility—financial reporting and internal control—the *latter* has a more pronounced effect on the degree of controller involvement.

Controller's Ability and Motivation

Since no attempt was made to study controller ability or motivation in a systematic way, what follows must be viewed as "impressionistic" evidence.

Technical competence was never an issue when executives attempted to explain why controllers were not more actively involved in business decision making. What was mentioned as important, and was sometimes missing, was a good understanding of the company's business and the ability to "speak the language of management." The chief executive officer at company 6, for example, described the controller

[21] Based on 14 observations, the coefficient of correlation between proportion of time spent by the corporate controller on external reporting (variable Q19) and degree of corporate controller involvement (variable Q6) is $-.09$, which would not be statistically significant below the .20 level had the observation been a statistical random sample (which they were not).

[22] Based on 18 observations, the relationship between strength of internal audit function (variable I2) and degree of corporate controller involvement (variable Q6) is 0.52, which would be statistically signficant below the .10 level had the observations been a statistical random sample (which they were not).

in these words: "He is smart and he is a good accountant. But he is not a management type. He leans heavily on accounting rather than on financial analysis and strategic decision making. He is stong in preparing numbers but weak in analyzing and using them."

In contrast, at company 9, the assistant controller described the corporate controller as follows: "He is not an accounting type. . . . He is proud of being a problem solver and a businessman." According to the president at company 1, "To be actively involved, the controller has to have a good knowledge of the business, a great deal of personal energy, be persuasive, and be recognized by peers as a capable person."

The controllers in this study also apparently differed in their level of motivation concerning involvement in business decisions, and this appeared to affect the level of actual involvement. For instance, the controller in company 5 had seen "bloody battles" fought earlier in the company's history between the controller and operating executives and refused to get involved in similar wars. On the other hand, in company 17, where management was not financially oriented, the controller attempted to educate the operating executives in financial matters to secure greater involvement.

The reasons for the apparent differences in ability and motivation are difficult to identify. They are not related to differences in background (for example, certified public accountants [CPA] versus non-CPA). Nor can the differences be attributed to the controller's career expectations. None of the corporate controllers stated a desire to move into operating management. All expected to remain in the finance and control area. The differences could not be traced to the controller's prior experience either. All but one of the corporate controllers had come up through controllership. Only in company 1 had the controller had previous operating experience. This experience apparently enhanced the controller's involvement, but others without such experience were equally or more involved.

Controller's Style

Although this study did not focus on personality traits or examine the quality of the interpersonal relationships between controllers and operating executives, one questionnaire measuring "conflict resolution style"[23] was used.

Hypothesis 4-8
The greater the corporate controller's reliance on the confrontation mode of conflict resolution, the greater the degree of his or her involvement in business decisions.

The essence of active controller involvement by the author's definition is the ability to recommend courses of action in making business decisions and the challenging of plans and actions of operating executives. For the controller to be

[23] Lawrence and Lorsch (1967).

able to do this, he or she must be able to deal with differences of opinion on issues that involve a great deal of judgment. Examples are questions such as the following: Is the sales forecast too optimistic? Are the receivables or inventory levels optimal? Is the promotion or advertising budget appropriate? Are the financial estimates in the capital investment plan or the new product development proposal realistic? It is one thing to be able to challenge management in the areas of accounting policy or internal control where defined rules and procedures clearly exist. It is quite another thing to be able to recommend and question business decisions and actions in areas where clear guidelines or answers do not exist.

Because of this, it is reasoned, active controller involvement in business decision making is facilitated if the controller is good at effectively resolving differences of opinion in such "gray" areas. Earlier research suggested the importance of adopting the "confrontation" mode ("by digging and digging the truth is discovered") rather than forcing ("might overcomes right") or "smoothing" ("let us agree to disagree") to effectively resolve such differences.[24]

When examined with quantitative data, the statistical association is of negligible magnitude, however.[25] All but one of the 14 corporate controllers for whom data are available indicated "confrontation" to be their primary mode of conflict resolution. Further, those more actively involved in decision making did not score significantly higher on the confrontation scale than others did.

Thus, variation in degree of corporate controller involvement is unrelated to the ability to confront because all corporate controllers scored high on the confrontation scale. The implications of this finding are explored further in the next chapter, which deals with division controller involvement within a company's division.

It should be noted that the unit of analysis in the next chapter is a *division* of a company rather than the company as a whole. In the chapter following the next, Chapter 6, analysis returns to the level of the company as intercompany differences in typical division controller involvement are examined. These changes in the level of analysis lead to some discontinuity in the focus of the discussion, but it makes sense to place Chapter 5 ahead of Chapter 6 because the material in the former provides useful background and orientation for the development of the latter. Those wishing to remain at the intercompany level of analysis, however, may proceed directly to Chapter 6 and pick up Chapter 5 later.

---

[24] Lawrence and Lorsch (1967).

[25] Based on 14 observations, the coefficient of correlation between corporate controller's reliance on confrontation mode in conflict resolution (variable Q17) and degree of corporate controller involvement (variable Q6) is .08, which would not be statistically significant below the .20 level had the observations been a statistical random sample (which they were not).

chapter 5

Degree of Controller Involvement in a Division of the Company

Because a *company* perspective rather than a *divisional* perspective was chosen as the primary focus for this study, data on variables and characteristics pertaining to a particular *division* of the company—the subject of this chapter—are limited. However, these data are now presented for three reasons. First, they allow some of the hypotheses developed in the previous chapter to be reexamined with a different set of data. Second, they permit discussion and exploration of the relationship between degree and scope of involvement, as defined presently (other chapters do not discuss scope of controller involvement). Finally, it is useful to discuss how controller involvement varies from division to division within the same company before ignoring such *intra*company variation to focus on *inter*company differences in the degree of *typical*[1] division controller involvement in the next chapter.

The phenomenon of controller involvement within a division of the company is in many ways similar to that of the corporate controller's involvement at headquarters. An important difference, however, is the fact that a division is not an independent organization—it is a part of the company. While the degree of divisional independence may vary, all divisions have by definition some linkages with the corporate headquarters. These linkages can influence division controller involvement.

To the extent that the phenomenon of controller involvement in a division parallels that of the corporate controller's involvement at headquarters, the hypotheses developed in the previous chapter apply. This chapter begins by reexamining

---

[1] Degree of typical division controller involvement is defined as the degree of controller involvement found most commonly in the company's divisions.

those hypotheses of Chapter 4 for which analogous division data are available. The corporate role in the division and associated consequences are considered later.

Limited data on controller involvement in 26 divisions of 13 companies are available. Controller involvement is measured in terms of *degree* of involvement, as defined previously, as well as in terms of the *scope* of involvement. The latter is defined as the number of key business decisions (that is, advertising, promotion, pricing) in which the division controller participates.[2] Although the degree and scope of division controller involvement are highly correlated,[3] they are examined separately to see if the various relationships obtained differ by degree versus scope of involvement.

REEXAMINATION OF HYPOTHESES IN CHAPTER 4

A summary of the hypotheses developed in Chapter 4 for which data on analogous divisional characteristics are available is shown in Exhibit 5-1, along with the results. The rationale for these hypotheses was presented in Chapter 4 and is not repeated here. When examined with the available data, the results are as follows.

Rate of Change of Division's Business Environment

The association between rate change of division's business environment and division controller involvement is in the predicted direction (positive) but is of negligible magnitude for both the degree or scope of involvement. This finding is consistent with that obtained earlier for the corresponding association between the degree of corporate controller involvement at headquarters and rate of change of corporate business environment.

Division Management's Expectations

As in the case of the corporate controller's involvement at headquarters, controller involvement in a division is positively associated with division management's expectations regarding such involvement. The results obtained for both degree and scope of involvement are in the predicted direction and the statistical associations

---

[2] The following business decisions were considered: advertising, promotion, distribution, acquisitions and mergers, new product development, capital investment, selection of executives outside the controllership area, credit policy, inventory policy, settling customer claims, and stopping customer deliveries. (Refer to variable Q8 in the appendix for further details.)

[3] Based on 22 observations, the coefficient of correlation between degree of division controller involvement (variable Q5) and scope of division controller involvement (variable Q8) is 0.55, which would be statistically significant at the .01 level had the observations been a statistical random sample (which they were not).

Exhibit 5-1 Divisional Characteristics and Division Controller Involvement
(A Reexamination of Hypotheses in Chapter 4 with Analogous Divisional Data)[a]

Hypothesis Number in Chapter 4	Analogous Divisional Characteristic	Hypothesized Direction of Association with Division Controller Involvement	Coefficient of Correlation Between Divisional Characteristic and Division Controller Involvement					
			Degree (Q5)			Scope (Q8)		
			Pearson Correlation Coefficient	Number of Observations	Magnitude of the Statistical Association[b]	Pearson Correlation Coefficient	Number of Observations	Magnitude of the Statistical Association[b]
4-1	Rate of change of division's business environment							
	Overall rate of change (Q12)	+	.20	19	Negligible	.13	22	Negligible
	Number of dimensions subject to rapid change (Q13)	+	.01	19	Negligible	.03	22	Negligible
	Composite index of rate of change (Q14)	+	.00	19	Negligible	.10	22	Negligible
4-6	Division management's expectations regarding division controller involvement (Q1)	+	0.59***	22	Strong	0.43**	25	Moderate
4-7	Proportion of time spent by division controller on external reporting (Q20)	–	0.01	21	Negligible	–.06	25	Negligible
4-8	Division controller's reliance on confrontation mode of conflict resolution (Q18)	+	0.10	22	Negligible	–.11	25	Negligible

[a]Numbers in parentheses refer to variable numbers in the Methodological Appendix.
[b]See Chapter 3, Presentation and Discussion of Results. Had the observations been a statistical random sample (which they were not), the p values would be as follows: *p < .20, **p < .10, ***p < .01.

are strong and moderate, respectively. Thus, management expectations are consistently related to controller involvement as predicted by role theory.[4]

Division Controller's Time Allocation to Areas of Responsibility

As in the case of the corporate controller's involvement at headquarters, controller involvement in a division is unrelated to the proportion of the controller's time spent on other responsibilities, that is, financial reporting. The same result is obtained for both degree and scope of division controller involvement.

Division Controller's Reliance on Confrontation in Conflict Resolution

As in the case of the corporate controller's involvement at headquarters, controller involvement in a division is unrelated to the extent of reliance on the confrontation mode in conflict resolution, for both degree and scope of involvement. The reason for this is that, as in the case of the corporate controllers, all division controllers in the study indicated extensive reliance on the confrontation mode in conflict resolution.

If these data are valid, they suggest that controllers who rise to senior levels of large, multidivisional U.S. companies predominantly rely on this mode of conflict resolution. Although this cannot be verified with available data, it may be that the ability to confront differences of opinion is so important to the controller's role at senior levels that those who are unable to do so simply do not rise to these levels. This speculation, based on the underlying rationale and results for Hypothesis 4-8, is worthy of exploration in future research because it has important implications for the training and development of controllers.

Summary

The results for degree versus scope of involvement are much the same. Thus, although degree and scope of involvement are conceptually distinct—the former captures intensity or depth of involvement, the latter suggests breadth of participation, that is, the number of key business decisions in which the controller is involved—the two are not only highly correlated but are also associated with various factors in similar ways. There is no further data on scope of involvement.

The findings on controller involvement in a division corroborate those obtained earlier on controller involvement at headquarters. Although analogous divisional data are not available on all the contextual factors considered in the previous chapter, no contradictory findings are obtained for those hypotheses in Chapter 4 that could be reexamined. The model of corporate controller involvement at head-

---

[4] Katz and Kahn (1978).

quarters in Exhibit 4-7 may thus be assumed to apply to division controller involvement as well. Substituting "division" for "corporate," Exhibit 4-7 becomes a model of division controller involvement.

The other major set of influences on the degree of division controller involvement, those relating to the corporate role in the division, may now be added.

CORPORATE ROLE IN THE DIVISION

Historically, the corporate role in divisional affairs has been described in terms of the degree of centralization or decentralization. By typical definition, an organization is considered "centralized to the extent that decisions are made at relatively high levels in the organization; decentralized to the extent that discretion and authority to make important decisions are delegated by top management to lower levels of executive authority."[5] More recently, however, the definition has been criticized for being simplistic. As one chief executive officer in this study pointed out, "It is our view that, although it is fashionable, we can't really speak in terms of the company's being centralized or decentralized. We decentralize those functions which it makes sense to decentralize, for example, pricing and product development in our case, because we can't get any economies of scale given our mix of businesses. For other functions, it clearly makes sense to centralize, for example, legal, treasury. Still other functions fall into the gray area—there are no clear-cut choices here; for example, our purchasing had been more centralized than it currently is."

This executive's point is that, by referring to a company as centralized or decentralized, the fact that some functions may be more or less centralized than others is overlooked. Others have found the dichotomy to be an inadequate representation of the constellation of factor (for example, management's operating philosophy and reliance on various organizational devices) that together influence the corporate management's role vis-à-vis the division.[6]

In this study the interest is in understanding how the corporate role in the division influences division controller involvement. Three types of corporate involvement in divisional affairs may be noted. In some cases there is limited direct contact (face to face or telephone) and little information exchange between corporate and division executives. What understanding corporate executives do gain from their limited involvement is not used as a basis for actively intervening in divisional affairs. In other cases there is greater contact and information exchange between corporate and division management. Corporate executives use the understanding gained from their involvement with the division to test division management's assumptions, to challenge them with penetrating questions, and to communicate corporate expectations regarding divisional performance. In still other cases, there is continuous contact and a great deal of information exchange between the corporate and the division executives. The corporate role goes beyond seeking

---

[5] Simon et al. (1954).
[6] Lorsch and Allen (1973).

information and challenging to direct involvement in division operations, including formulation of divisional policy, decision making, and decision implementation.

As the corporate role in the division increases, division controller involvement could be increasingly influenced by corporate management. At company 5, for example, a recently appointed chief operating officer was described by several executives as being both actively involved in divisional operations and financially oriented. In the words of the chief financial officer, "He relies heavily on financial information, has a fantastic memory for faces and facts, and believes in face-to-face and phone discussions." This financially oriented chief operating officer personally visited all company divisions for the monthly performance reviews and was actively involved in managing one division that was in financial difficulty. His "demand" for financial information and analysis and the expectation that the division controllers play a more active role led to the increased involvement of several division controllers and to the replacement of one. According to the chief operating officer, "When I came here, the general manager of the_____ division was flying by the seat of his pants. I got him a strong controller."

The corporate management at company 2 was also actively involved in the operations of several divisions. The chief operating officer was in *daily* contact with the largest division located 300 miles away. A group vice president closely controlled five divisions and an executive vice president eight others. However, because the chief executive officer and other key corporate executives were not financially oriented, no additional demand for financial information and analysis was generated, and there was no greater expectation regarding division controller involvement. Such involvement was therefore unaffected.

The preceding illustrates that corporate involvement in the division may influence the degree of division controller involvement if the corporate involvement generates an additional demand for financial information and analysis or the expectation of greater division controller involvement. This influence can also be represented by appropriately modifying Exhibit 4-7. As has been mentioned, substituting "division" for "corporate" makes the exhibit a model of how divisional contextual factors influence division controller involvement. The influence of the corporate role may be added by replacing the term "division management" with the phrase "corporate and division management" when the degree of corporate involvement in the division is high.

Since the corporate role in the division can influence the degree of division controller involvement, the reasons for varying degrees of corporate involvement in the division are now considered.

REASONS FOR VARYING DEGREES OF CORPORATE INVOLVEMENT IN THE DIVISION

A summary of various factors influencing the degree of corporate involvement in the division appears in Exhibit 5-2. Because quantitative data are not available, the discussion that follows is purely qualitative in nature. Reliance is on interview

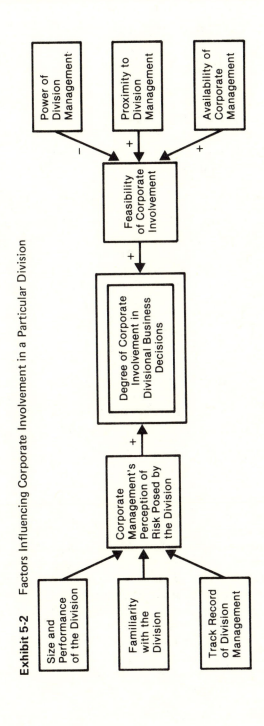

Exhibit 5-2   Factors Influencing Corporate Involvement in a Particular Division

quotations rather than on statistical correlations to indicate the relationships inferred.

Corporate Management's Perception of Risk Posed by the Division

Among the variables that influence corporate management's perception of risk posed by the division are the following: size and performance of the division, familiarity with the division's business, and track record of division management. Although interrelated, each is discussed separately for convenience of discussion. Their combined effects are considered later.

Size and performance.   All other things being the same, larger divisions pose greater risk to corporate top management. They use a proportionately greater amount of corporate resources. Since more is at stake in the larger division, corporate management perceives the need to watch it more carefully. The same is true of the poorly performing division. When performance falls below corporate expectations, corporate involvement usually increases. For example, according to the controller of a division of company 19, which was losing money heavily, "Top management is greatly involved in operations (for example, 'What are you doing with customer X or distributor Y? How many people are required in packaging?''). The group vice president is even more involved. He is extremely cost conscious and we have had trouble getting increases in staff."

More interesting, and perhaps less obvious, is the case of the *high*-performing division receiving corporate attention. According to the controller of a small- to moderate-sized division of company 8, for example, "For the first time in its history, this division was the primary contributor to the group's sales and earnings records of last year. Since our division is more important now, corporate wants to know more about us. They are becoming more actively involved." Thus, a change in performance far below *or* far above prior expectations may produce increased corporate involvement.

Familiarity with the division's business.   A somewhat analogous relationship occurs with respect to corporate management's familiarity with the division's business. If top management is well acquainted with a particular division's business (either because they came up through that division or because of prior experience with that type of business in another division or company), the likelihood of involvement is great. This may be attributed to the proverbial "inability to let go." Because of corporate management's expertise in the business, these people tend to seek information, ask questions, and propose solutions in ways that they find difficulty to do in divisions less familiar to them.

Less obvious is the case of involvement in a division whose business is *not* familiar to corporate management. According to the president of the chemical division at company 24, for instance, "Corporate management is excessively involved in this division because the recently appointed chief operating officer came up through the _____ division [completely unrelated to chemicals]. He wants to understand this business." Thus, both high and low degrees of familiarity may produce increased corporate involvement, depending on other factors. As one corporate controller explained, "Any aberrational situation increases attention, for example, large or small profits, high or low technology. It is normalcy or business as usual that lowers involvement."

Track record of division management.   All other things being the same, corporate management tends to be more involved with division management who have not established a proven track record. The most common instances of such involvement are with newly appointed management in existing divisions or with existing management of acquired divisions. At a division of company 15, for example, where two division general managers had been replaced in the previous three years, the incumbent stated, "The previous DGMs were unable or unwilling to cut staff. I began to cut costs the day I got in. . . . The only way to build credibility is to produce *results*—deliver in deeds, not in words. It takes time, but I am showing results. Corporate management's involvement is decreasing simultaneously."

Feasibility of Corporate Involvement

Corporate involvement is also conditioned by the feasibility of such involvement. Among other factors, the following appear to be important: power and proximity of division management and availability of corporate management.

Power of division management.   In several divisions visited division management was "left alone" by corporate executives because of a "strong" or "powerful" division general manager. A division general manager in company 11 was described as follows by a corporate executive: "We have to leave him alone because he is a strong personality. He commands power because the division's business relies on a few key customers and he controls them. If he goes, they go." Thus, although the division general manager was described as a "strong personality," his source of power and the reason he was "left alone" was his control over the crucial customers. The same was true of one division general manager in company 4 and another in company 7. Although the autonomy they enjoyed was attributed to their "strong personality" by fellow executives, their source of power in fact seemed to be the perception of their unique contribution to the corporation. In company 4 the executive had expert know-how in a very specialized business. In company 7 the executive had a long history of producing results when "left alone." According to him, "We run our own show. We don't talk to people across the hall [corporate staff]. Our main contact at the corporate level is the chief executive officer, and he doesn't get too involved. The previous chief executive officer was driving me crazy with a lot of interference."

Proximity.   As the quote indicates, proximity to corporate management does not automatically result in a high degree of corporate involvement in division management. It does, however, *facilitate* such involvement when other factors encourage it. At company 15, for example, a division located at corporate headquarters attributed poor performance to "excessive interference from corporate management because they happen to be here." Corporate management was considering moving the division management out of the corporate headquarters building to eliminate this perceived problem.

At company 24 somewhat the opposite had occurred. Because top management wanted to become more acquainted with an important division located far from corporate headquarters, divisional headquarters were moved into the corporate office at an opportune time, that is, construction of a new headquarters office complex that just "happened to have a lot of extra space!"

Availability of corporate management. Even if other factors point toward corporate involvement, it may not take place simply because of preoccupation with other matters. At company 7, for instance, the chief financial officer perceived a need for greater involvement with the divisions in the financial area but was not able to do so because other more pressing matters were taking up all his time. In his words, "When I came on board two years ago, the company's balance sheet was in bad shape on account of certain acquisitions that didn't fit well, financially speaking. My first task was to divest the company of them and restructure the company's debt. This has kept me busy until now."

Combined Effects

For ease of presentation the preceding discussion considered factors influencing corporate involvement in the division one at a time (Exhibit 5-2). In reality, of course, involvement is the result of the combined effect of these and other factors that are hard to disentangle. A couple of examples will illustrate what happens in actual practice.

In the case of company 7, just cited, one reason that the chief financial officer was not more actively involved was his preoccupation with divestitures. But other reasons were the basic philosophy of a "holding company" practiced by the chief executive officer and the fact that the principal division's general manager exercised a great deal of power in the corporation and resented "corporate interference" (see illustration under Power of Division Management).

The following changes occurred at another company. As an acquired division that was originally a small piece of the corporate pie grew and became the company's biggest and most profitable division, corporate management paid increasing attention to it. Because of the division's increasing size and strong performance, corporate management became highly dependent on the division. At the same time, top management felt that it was now more vulnerable to the division because of its relative unfamiliarity with the division's business. In an effort to facilitate better understanding of the division and its business, corporate management wanted to move divisional offices located in the South to corporate headquarters in the

Northeast. At the time of the research visit, the move was being strongly resisted by a division management team that had acquired considerable prestige and power in the corporation.

Although the corporate role in the division varies from division to division within the same company, there are also important company-to-company differences. These differences, and the associated consequences for typical divisional controller involvement in the company, are the subject of the next chapter.

chapter 6

Degree of Typical Division Controller Involvement in the Company

As in the two previous chapters, the hypotheses developed and examined in this chapter explore the relationships between various contextual factors and the degree of controller involvement. Chapter 4 considered the influence of the company's environment, business, and corporate management on the degree of corporate controller involvement at headquarters. These contextual variables are considered here again with regard to the extent that they influence the degree of *typical*[1] division controller involvement in the company. Chapter 5 described how the corporate role varies from division to division within the same company and mentioned the associated consequences for division controller involvement. This chapter is concerned with *inter*company, rather than *intra*company, differences. Accordingly, the typical corporate posture vis-à-vis the divisions and the associated consequences for typical division controller involvement in the company are considered. Because both corporate management and the corporate controller have linkages with the division, both are examined.

The chapter begins with hypotheses dealing with the influence of the company's environmental and business characteristics on the degree of typical division controller involvement in the company. The influence of corporate management characteristics is considered next, followed by an examination of the relationships between corporate controller characteristics and the degree of typical division controller involvement.

[1] Defined as the degree of division controller involvement most prevalent in the company as a whole. See variable Q7 in the Methodological Appendix for details concerning the measurement of this variable.

ENVIRONMENTAL AND BUSINESS CHARACTERISTICS AND TYPICAL DIVISION CONTROLLER INVOLVEMENT

Companies differ in the rapidity with which their business environments change, in the degree of operating interdependence between their business divisions, and in the extent to which financial analysis and control are critical in these particular operating environments. Hypotheses relating each of these factors and the degree of corporate controller involvement at headquarters were developed and examined in Chapter 4. Analogous hypotheses connecting these contextual variables and the degree of typical division controller involvement in the company are summarized in Exhibit 6-1, along with the data used to examine them. The rationale underlying these hypotheses parallels that given for the corresponding hypotheses in Chapter 4 and is not repeated here.

Rate of Change of Corporate Business Environment

Hypothesis 6-1
The greater the rate of change of the corporate business environment, the higher the degree of typical division controller involvement.

The magnitude of the statistical association is negligible (Exhibit 6-1). The result is consistent with that obtained for the analogous hypothesis in Chapter 4. Thus, when examined with statistical data, rate of change of the corporate business environment is unrelated to controller involvement at both the corporate and the division levels.

Degree of Operating Interdependence

Hypothesis 6-2
The greater the degree of operating interdependence within the company, the greater the degree of typical division controller involvement.

Again, the magnitude of the statistical association is negligible (Exhibit 6-1). Because a weak association exists for the analogous hypothesis in Chapter 4, two possibilities exist. The first is that the relationship of operating interdependence and controller involvement is a tenuous one. The second possibility is that company operating interdependence influences controller involvement at the corporate level but not at the divisional level. The two interpretations are not necessarily inconsistent and deserve further exploration in future research.

Criticality of Financial Analysis and Control

Hypothesis 6-3
The greater the importance of financial analysis and control to business success, the higher the degree of typical division controller involvement.

Higher capital intensity and working capital intensity, and lower profit margin, are predicted to be associated with a higher degree of typical division controller involvement. When examined with quantitative data, the association for working asset intensity is moderate and the other two are of negligible magnitude (Exhibit 6-1).

In Chapter 4 the corporate controller's involvement at headquarters was found to be associated with capital asset intensity but not with working asset intensity. This may be because decisions most affecting the management of working assets typically reside at the division level in large, multidivisional companies. As such, criticality of working asset management is associated with a higher degree of controller involvement at the division level but not at corporate headquarters.

The findings for capital asset intensity are just the opposite, although the association is weak. They indicate that the criticality of capital asset management is not associated with higher degree of controller involvement in the divisions but, rather, at corporate headquarters. This may be because, although capital investment proposals emanate in the divisions, they are typically actively reviewed at headquarters. To the extent that such decisions are critical for a company, the corporate headquarters is more actively involved in these decisions, leading to greater corporate controller involvement at headquarters.

CORPORATE MANAGEMENT CHARACTERISTICS AND TYPICAL DIVISION CONTROLLER INVOLVEMENT

Corporate managements differ in their financial background, financial orientation, expectations regarding division controller involvement, operating style, and management philosophy. Five hypotheses are developed and examined to see how each of these factors influence the degree of typical division controller involvement in the company (see Exhibit 6-2).

Hypothesis 6-4
The greater the degree of corporate management's financial background, the greater the degree of typical division controller involvement.

There appears to be no prior research to support this hypothesis. However, because controller involvement is related to the financial backgrounds of management at the same level (Chapter 4), the "interlevel" effects are being examined. Although a financially trained corporate management dampens the degree of

Exhibit 6-1 Examination of Hypotheses Relating Environmental and Business Characteristics and Degree of Typical Division Controller Involvement in Business Decisions (Q7)[a]

Hypothesis Number	Contextual Variable	Hypothesized Direction of Association Between Contextual Variable and Degree of Typical Division Controller Involvement (Q7)	Pearson Correlation Coefficient	Number of Observations	Magnitude of the Statistical Association[b]
6-1	Rate of change of corporate business environment				
	Overall rate of change (Q9)	+	.16	16	Negligible
	Number of environmental dimensions subject to rapid change (Q10)	+	.01	16	Negligible
	Composite index of environmental change (Q11)	+	.09	16	Negligible
6-2	Company operating interdependence (D3)	+	.07	24	Negligible
6-3	Criticality of financial analysis and control				
	Capital asset intensity (D6)	+	.05	24	Negligible
	Working asset intensity (D7)	+	.35**	24	Moderate
	Operating margin (D8)	−	-.01	23	Negligible

[a]Numbers in parentheses refer to variable numbers in the Methodological Appendix.

[b]See Chapter 3, Presentation and Discussion of Results. Had the observations been a statistical random sample (which they were not), the p values would be as follows: $*p < .20$, $**p < .10$, $***p < .01$.

Exhibit 6-2 Examination of Hypotheses on Corporate Management Characteristics and Degree of Typical Division Controller Involvement[a]

Hypothesis Number	Characteristic of Corporate Management	Hypothesized Direction of Association Between Characteristic and Degree of Typical Division Controller Involvement	Pearson Correlation Coefficient	Number of Observations	Magnitude of the Statistical Association[b]
6-4	Financial ability				
	CEO has financial background (D-4)	+	0.10	23	Negligible
	Percentage of senior corporate executives with financial background (D5)	+	−0.24	23	Negligible
6-5	Financial orientation (I8)	+	0.52***	23	Strong
6-6	Expectations regarding typical division controller involvement (Q3)	+	0.57**	16	Moderate
6-7	Emphasis on planning, budgeting, and capital expenditure review (Q15)	+	0.53***	22	Strong
6-8	Emphasis on controllership– line transfers (I7)	+	0.42**	22	Moderate

[a]Numbers in parentheses refer to variable numbers in the Methodological Appendix.

[b]See Chapter 3, Presentation and Discussion of Results. Had the observations been a statistical random sample (which they were not), the p values would be as follows: *$p < .20$, **$p < .10$, ***$p < .01$.

controller involvement at headquarters, the opposite effect may be expected on controller involvement in the divisions for the following reason. The "dampening effect" at headquarters is attributed to financially trained corporate management acting as its own "controller." There is no reason to expect such training at the corporate level to "drive out" division controller involvement in typical *divisional* business decisions. Rather, a financially trained corporate management may provide additional status to financial personnel in the company. If so, such status may enhance controller involvement in the company's divisions.

Two measures are used for corporate management's financial background—the extent to which the chief executive officer is financially trained and the percentage of senior corporate executives with financial background. When examined with these data, the statistical associations are of negligible magnitude (Exhibit 6-2). This finding, along with the earlier result in Chapter 4, suggests that corporate management's financial ability has some local effect (corporate controller's involvement) but no significant interlevel effect (division controller involvement).

Hypothesis 6-5
The greater the degree of corporate management's financial *orientation,* the greater the degree of typical division controller involvement.

By the definition given in Chapter 4, management that is financially oriented emphasizes financial information and analysis in its management approach. If corporate management has this orientation, it will request a great deal of such information and analysis from the divisions. This creates an opportunity for greater controller involvement at the division level.

When examined with the quantitative data, the statistical association is strong (Exhibit 6-2). The following quotations illustrate how corporate management's financial orientation may help to induce a similar orientation in division management and increase the potential for division controller involvement. According to the chief financial officer at company 15, "Every one of our division general managers is highly financially oriented. When the chief executive officer [a financially oriented executive] took over many years ago, it wasn't so. Over the years our managers have learned to pay attention to the numbers." At company 19 a similar change occurred after the chief executive officer became financially oriented as a result of a financial crisis. Said the chief executive officer (in 1977), "Our people were not prepared to deal with it [the financial crisis in 1974-1975]. Operating managers couldn't cope because they didn't understand the fundamentals of financial control. . . . As a result of our emphasis on monthly asset management reviews where inventories, receivables, and cost reductions are discussed, division management has become much more financially oriented."

The following comment by a division manager in company 14, whose corporate management is highly financially oriented, illustrates how such orientation in division management may lead to a greater degree of involvement for the division controller: "Before going to corporate headquarters, I always ask my controller, 'What do you think are some of the things they may be concerned about?' My controller may say, 'Our estimate for next month is. . . . We are having difficulty because. . . . This is what I feel we should tell corporate'. . . ."

Management's Expectations

Hypothesis 6-6
The higher the corporate management's expectations regarding division controller involvement, the greater the degree of actual involvement.

As discussed earlier, expectations of local management regarding controller involvement are consistently and positively related to the degree of actual involvement. All previously reported data—on controller involvement at corporate headquarters and in a particular division of the company—shows this consistently. Although division controllers do not work directly for corporate management, the latter's expectations could be important because of their hierarchical position and opportunity to "set the tone" of the organization.

There is a moderate statistical association as shown in Exhibit 6-2. Thus, corporate management's expectations regarding controller involvement are related not only to the degree of corporate controller involvement at headquarters but also to the degree of controller involvement in the company's divisions.

Operating Style

Hypothesis 6-7
The greater the corporate management emphasis on the company's financial planning, budgeting, and capital expenditure review system, the greater the degree of typical division controller involvement.

Corporate managements differ in the extent to which they rely on these systems to manage corporate-division relationships.[2] Since controllers play an important role in the planning, budgeting, and capital expenditure review process, top management's emphasis on these activities in their dealings with the divisions would generate increased opportunity for division controller involvement in the company. The statistical association obtained using quantitative data is strong (Exhibit 6-2).

Management Philosophy

Hypothesis 6-8
The greater the corporate management emphasis on controllership to line transfers, the greater the degree of typical division controller involvement.

The traditional distinction between "line" and "staff" is discussed in Chapter 1. Corporate management of the companies studied differ in the degree to which they

[2] Lorsch and Allen (1973).

emphasize this distinction. In some the line-staff distinction is emphasized along traditional lines: the line is responsible for results, the staff for advice and services. In others the staff role receives greater emphasis as illustrated by the following examples.

In company 8 the chief operating officer had this comment: "We expect and we are willing to live with a certain amount of line-staff friction. We watch for such friction to keep a balance between line and staff. For example, line can protest if staff is unreasonable, but they cannot jump the system. On the other hand, if complaints crop up from more than one division about a particular staff department or person, we will call the staff in and ask, 'What's going on?' The key is that we have a 'bubble-up' system—bitching is permitted." At company 23, where the staff role is also emphasized, the chief financial officer stated, "Ten years ago you could get around the staff in this company. Now the chief executive and other key operating officers are involved with the staff, and today it is simply not possible for operating executives to do this—the chief operating officer and the chief executive officer ask line managers what the staff said." According to the vice president of planning, "The company used to have weak staff in the 1960s. Now we have a strong line and a strong staff."

Management's emphasis on the line-staff distinction may be gauged by examining the career paths of executives in line and staff positions. In some companies there are few controllership to line transfers, for example. In others such transfer are more prevalent. To the extent that such transfers are common, the distinction between line and staff blurs, and greater controller involvement in decision making is likely to occur under these conditions. There is a moderate statistical association when the hypothesis is examined with quantitative data (Exhibit 6-2). Various corporate controller characteristics and related consequences for controller involvement in the divisions are now examined.

CORPORATE CONTROLLER CHARACTERISTICS AND TYPICAL DIVISION CONTROLLER INVOLVEMENT

In the companies studied the division controllers typically report directly to their local management with a technical or functional responsibility to the corporate controller. The degree of the corporate controller's formal authority over the division controllers varies considerably, however, as do other corporate controller characteristics. Five hypotheses are developed and examined to study how each of these characteristics is related to the degree of typical division controller involvement in the company (see Exhibit 6-3).

Hypothesis 6-9
The greater the degree of formal authority of the corporate controller over the division controllers, the lower the degree of typical division controller involvement.

Exhibit 6-3 Examination of Hypothesis on Corporate Controller Characteristics and Degree of Typical Division Controller Involvement[a]

Hypothesis Number	Corporate Controller Characteristics	Hypothesized Direction of Association Between Characteristic and Degree of Typical Division Controller Involvement	Pearson Correlation Coefficient	Number of Observations	Magnitude of the Statistical Association[b]
6-9	Degree of corporate controller's formal authority over division controllers (Q16)	−	.12	15	Negligible
6-10	Corporate controller's expectations regarding division controller involvement (Q4)	+	.23	16	Negligible
6-11	Corporate controller's emphasis on the service role in dealing with management				
	Degree of corporate controller's own involvement in business decisions at corporate headquarters (Q6)	+	0.35*	21	Weak
	Proportion of time spent by the corporate controller's headquarters	+	0.45**	14	Moderate

Exhibit 6-3 (continued)

Hypothesis Number	Corporate Controller Characteristics	Hypothesized Direction of Association Between Characteristic and Degree Typical Division Controller Involvement	Correlation Coefficient	Number of Observations	Magnitude of the Statistical Association[b]
	staff on division management reports and requests				
6-12	Corporate controller's current emphasis on personnel development				
	Own involvement in personnel development (I5)	+	−.01	23	Negligible
	Personnel executives assigned to controllership (I4)	+	.15	24	Negligible
	Audit as training ground (I3)	+	−.06	19	Negligible
6-13	Duration of sustained emphasis on development of controllership personnel (I6)	+	0.55***	22	Strong

[a]Numbers in parentheses refer to variable numbers in the Methodological Appendix.

[b]See Chapter 3, Presentation and Discussion of Results. Had the observations been a statistical random sample (which they were not) the p values would be as follows: *$p < .20$, **$p < .10$, ***$p < .01$.

Since the division controllers report to the corporate controller in the areas of "technical" responsibility—bookkeeping, adherence to corporate accounting policy, and auditing procedures—these responsibilities may receive increasing emphasis as the extent of formal authority of the corporate controller over the division controllers increases. The responsibility for contributing to the divisional business decisions—the "service" role—would consequently suffer.

The statistical association is of a negligible magnitude (Exhibit 6-3). The next hypothesis examines the relationship between corporate controller's expectations regarding division controller involvement in business decisions and actual involvement.

Expectations Regarding Division Controller Involvement

Hypothesis 6-10

The higher the corporate controller's expectations regarding typical division controller involvement, the higher the actual degree of typical involvement.

The hypothesis is derived from role theory,[3] as previously discussed. Because the corporate controller is one of the "role senders" when the division controller is the focal role, the corporate controller's expectations should influence division controller involvement.

The statistical association is of a negligible magnitude, however (Exhibit 6-3). The finding has interesting implications because it indicates that, although corporate management expectations regarding division controller involvement are moderately related to the actual degree of typical involvement (Hypothesis 6-6), the corporate controller's expectations are not.

Emphasis on the Service Role

Hypothesis 6-11

The greater the corporate controller's emphasis on the service role in dealings with division management, the greater the degree of typical division controller involvement.

The degree of actual emphasis placed by the corporate controller on the technical versus the service aspects of controllership varies from company to company. To the extent that the corporate controller emphasizes the service role, the division controller involvement in business decisions may be facilitated.

Two surrogate measures are used to capture differences in the degree to which the corporate controller emphasizes the service role: the degree of the corporate controller's own involvement in business decisions and the proportion of time spent

[3] Katz and Kahn (1978).

by the corporate controller's corporate staff on division management's reports and requests. The corresponding statistical associations are of weak and moderate magnitude, respectively (Exhibit 6-3). Thus, the corporate controller's emphasis on the service role in dealings with management appear to be more important than his or her degree of formal authority, or expectations, as far as the consequences for division controller involvement are concerned.

Emphasis on Human Resource Development

Hypothesis 6-12
The greater the corporate controller's emphasis on human resource development, the greater the degree of typical division controller involvement.

Companies differ in the extent to which the corporate controller and his or her staff devote attention and effort to the development of controllership personnel within the company. In some the corporate controller devotes a great deal of time and energy to matters concerning the selection, training, and development of personnel. Sometimes there is a senior executive reporting directly to the corporate controller engaged full time in these activities. The emphasis placed on the corporate internal audit department as a "training ground" for future managers also varies from company to company. In some, personnel with high potential are recruited into the corporate internal audit department and then are "farmed out" to the divisions on a planned basis within two to five years. Such an assignment pattern is viewed as providing a training opportunity because it gives the recruits a good overview of corporate operations and an opportunity to communicate with managers in various field locations. In other companies there is little movement of personnel from the corporate internal audit department on a planned basis—the department is staffed primarily with "career auditors."

Since such training and development activities are intended to increase the competence of personnel and broaden their outlook and understanding of business issues, they could facilitate greater involvement in business decisions.

Three surrogate measures are used for the corporate controller's emphasis on human resource development: the proportion of the corporate controller's own time spent on personnel development, the extent to which one or more other senior executives are engaged full time in these activities, and the extent to which the corporate internal audit department is used as a training ground. The statistical associations are of negligible magnitude for all three sets of data (Exhibit 6-3).

One reason for this finding may be that it takes a long period of time before attention to training and development bears fruit. In several companies visited, such activities had been started relatively recently, and the long lead time between action and effect may account for the results. If so, the associations should be stronger for the following hypothesis.

Period of Sustained Emphasis on Development of Controllership Personnel

Hypothesis 6-13
The longer the period of sustained emphasis on development of controllership personnel, the greater the degree of typical division controller involvement.

In some companies, development of controllership personnel has been emphasized over a long period of time, by one of more corporate controllers. In others, it has received more recent attention. In still others, such activities had never been

Exhibit 6-4   Contextual Factors and Degree of Typical Division Controller Involvement in the Company

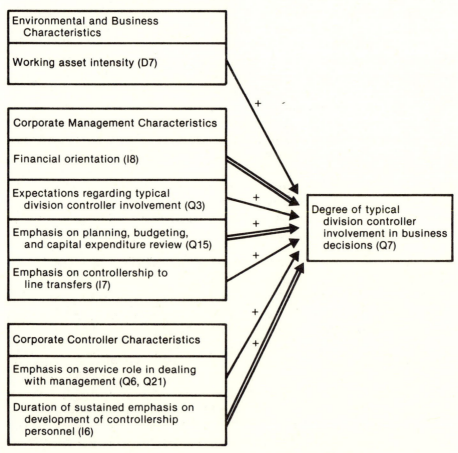

Numbers in parentheses refer to variables in the Methodological Appendix. Solid lines represent moderate statistical associations. Double solid lines represent strong statistical associations.

emphasized. The longer the duration of sustained emphasis on human resource development, the greater the likelihood of impact on controller involvement.

When examined with the quantitative data, the statistical association is strong (Exhibit 6-3). Thus, the evidence suggests that emphasis on human resource development activities is related to degree of division controller involvement, but it takes a long period of such emphasis—five to ten years according to the measurements—before the benefits are realized. The finding has important practical implications to be discussed in Chapter 8.

A summary of how various environmental, business, corporate management, and corporate controller characteristics influence the degree of typical division controller involvement appears in Exhibit 6-4. The next part of the book considers the implications of the study findings for future research, theory, and practice.

part III

Implications for Theory and Practice

Part I of this book explained why the question of controller involvement is of considerable practical importance and examined the potential benefits and costs associated with heightened controller involvement. Part II considered the influence of various contextual factors on controller involvement, and models were developed indicating the magnitude of the association among characteristics of the company's environment, business, and management and the degree of controller involvement at the corporate and division levels of the company. In Part III, the implications of this work for theory and practice are considered.

Although focused on the question of controller involvement in business decisions, the theoretical implications of this work are broader than this for two main reasons. First, as was pointed out in Chapter 1, what is learned about the controller's role in management has relevance to other staff roles now increasingly facing the same dilemma that the controllers have experienced for a long time. Second, this research was conducted using a conceptual framework derived not only from earlier work on controller involvement but also on other research and theory in the field of organizational behavior, for example, the contingency theory of organization and role theory. As such, the findings have general implications for the development of theory and the conduct of research in organizational behavior. These implications are discussed in Chapter 7. A conceptual framework for examining effective performance of staff roles in management is developed. A new conceptualization of organizational effectiveness is also presented. The chapter concludes by highlighting certain findings uncovered in this study that raise important practical questions that remain unanswered on the basis of the available evidence.

In discussing the implications of the work for practical affairs (Chapter 8), the role taken is that of a consultant rather than that of a researcher or scholar. In the latter role, adopted throughout the book up to that point, the discussion is limited to describing and analyzing trends and relationships found in the particular companies studied. But what do these data—these "facts," if you will—mean for the practitioner?

Managers seek information and analysis as a basis for action, and action is based not only on questions of fact (for example, why and how does the controller's role vary from company to company and what are the related consequences?) but also on questions of value and judgment[1] (that is, what *should* the controller's role be in *our* company?). To be of help to the practitioner, therefore, an attempt is made to be provocative in Chapter 8—by raising questions, offering recommendations, and generally sharing judgments about the various issues considered. As such, reliance is not only on the study findings but also on personal insights and experience.

The topics covered in this last chapter include the question of what the role of the division controllers should be in a given company and the analogous question of what the role of the corporate controller at headquarters should be. Recommendations for those seeking to develop "strong" controllers, that is, controllers able to remain actively involved in business decisions while retaining a sense of objectivity and independence from management, are presented. Implications for other staff roles in management are also considered.

[1] Simon (1945), p. 46.

chapter 7

Implications for Research and Theory

Because this book uses a conceptual framework based on earlier research and theory, it is now possible to review the findings in light of this earlier work and examine the implications for future research and theory. The findings relating to prior research on controller involvement are reviewed first. Broader implications for descriptive organization theory are considered next. Included are suggested extensions to role theory and the contingency theory of organization.

Following this the chapter is devoted to a discussion of the implications of the book for prescriptive organization theory. Such theories are what practitioners seek in their efforts to better manage their affairs. Unfortunately that is what they generally don't get from much current research and theorizing. The reasons for this disturbing gap between theory and practice are identified, and a conceptual framework for examining staff effectiveness is developed. Also included is a discussion of how the findings of this study, together with earlier evidence from other areas of organizational research, lead to a new conceptualization of the concept of organizational effectiveness. The chapter closes with some important questions uncovered here that cannot be answered on the basis of the available evidence.

RESEARCH ON CONTROLLER INVOLVEMENT

As was discussed in Chapter 1, two previous studies have indicated that controller involvement may be adversely affected by the bookkeeping activities, which are clearly defined and programmed to a rigid schedule. In contrast, service activities, offering the opportunity for involvement in business decisions, are neither well defined nor rigidly programmed and are consequently neglected. To overcome this difficulty, one study[1] recommended a separation of the bookkeeping and service functions to ensure that sufficient attention is paid to the latter. Based on similar reasoning, a more recent study suggested that controller involvement may be facilitated if the bookkeeping activities are computerized, thus allowing more time for the service function:

> Unfortunately, no data measuring computerization of accounts and system effectiveness was collected. The advent of effective computerized accounting systems may however be a major factor influencing the role of the accountant. Where such changes have taken place, then the bookkeeping activities and the demands of the work flow may be less significant, allowing the accountant greater time to develop the service activities.[2]

Research for this book, conducted at about the same time, did not directly measure the extent of computerization either. But the percentage of time that the controller spent on the external reporting activities was measured. The greater the preoccupation with these activities, it was reasoned, the lesser the time available for service to management and the lower the degree of controller involvement. However, this relationship was not obtained for either the degree of corporate controller involvement at headquarters (Hypothesis 4-7) or for the degree or scope of division controller involvement (Exhibit 5-1, Hypothesis 4-7).

These data suggest that time available for service to management is not very important to the question of controller involvement. Neither the degree of involvement, as captured by the recommending of action and/or the challenging of operating executives, nor the scope of involvement, that is, the number of key business decisions in which the controller participates, is related to the time available for service to management. Other factors, shown in the various models of controller involvement developed in this study, are more important.

The findings of this study bearing on the influence of management's expectations corroborate those obtained by Hopper[3]—the combined results of these two studies support role theory.[4] However, other factors are also important in explaining controller involvement. These results are now reviewed in light of the earlier organization theory and research on which this study attempted to build.

This earlier work is of two vintages. Some of it, that is, role theory, is concerned principally with description and explanation of the phenomenon under investigation. Other work, that is, contingency theory of organization, is also directed at the question of *effectiveness* and includes prescriptions for improving performance. Implications for descriptive organization theory are considered first. Implications for prescriptive theory follow.

[1] Simon, et al. (1954).
[2] Hopper (1978), p. 144.
[3] Hopper (1978).
[4] Katz and Kahn (1978), Chap. 7.

IMPLICATIONS FOR DESCRIPTIVE
ORGANIZATION THEORY

There are two ways in which descriptive organization theory may be classified. One is a classification indicating whether or not the object of investigation—the "unit of analysis"—is an individual or group within the organization or the total organization. These perspectives are commonly referred to as "micro" (individual and group) versus "macro" (organizational). The results of this study may be reviewed from both perspectives. Two of the models developed focus on an aspect of individual behavior, for example, degree of controller involvement at headquarters (Chapter 4) and in a division (Chapter 5), and are thus "micro" in their perspective. The third model focuses on an attribute of the total organization, that is, the degree of *typical* division controller involvement in the company (Chapter 6), and thus belongs to the "macro" school.

Organization theory and research also differ in the extent to which they rely on "internal" versus "external" factors in explaining behavior—be it that of an individual or an organization. In the case of "micro" theories, for example, achievement theory[5] and trait theory[6] rely primarily on internal factors—the individual's need for achievement and personality traits—to explain individual behavior. Other studies have considered the importance of external factors as well, for example, role theory.[7] In the case of work conducted with a "macro" perspective, studies have traditionally considered internal factors, relating one attribute of the organization (such as size or technology) to another (such as span of control or formality of structure).[8] More recent work examines the influence on the organization of factors external to it, for example, contingency theory of organization.[9]

This book is concerned mainly with how factors external to the object of inquiry—the controllers—influence one aspect of individual and organizational behavior—the degree of controller or typical controller involvement in business decision making. In general, the findings support a situational perspective on organizational behavior. The results indicate that individual controller involvement, as well as *typical* controller involvement in the company, are systematically related to factors external to the controllers, that is, to characteristics of the company's environment, business, and management. These results are now reviewed, first from the perspective of role theory and then from the perspective of the contingency theory of organization.

Implications for Role Theory

As was mentioned, the results in Chapters 4 and 5 are consistent with role theory. (See Exhibit 4-7 and 5-1 for a summary of the findings.) Behavior of the individual in the focal role—the controller—is consistently and positively related to

[5] McClelland (1961).
[6] Jenkins (1947).
[7] Katz and Kahn (1978).
[8] Hall (1972).
[9] Thompson (1967); Lawrence and Lorsch (1967).

the expectations of the role senders—the management. This relationship is shown as "arrow 1" in the conceptual framework of role theory shown in Exhibit 7-1. Certain attributes of the environment and the business—the situational factors—are also related to role sender's (management's) expectations, as predicted by role theory and depicted as "arrow 2" in Exhibit 7-1. (See Exhibit 4-9 for a summary of these results.)

However, situational factors not only influence role behavior indirectly—via role sender's expectations as shown in Exhibit 7-1—but directly as well, as evident from the results obtained for the company's capital asset intensity and operating interdependence (Exhibit 4-7). Role sender's attributes other than expectations, that is, management's financial ability and orientation, also influence behavior in the focal role, that is, controller involvement. It should be noted that these role sender characteristics are directly related to role behavior (Exhibit 4-7) and are unrelated to role sender's expectations (Exhibit 4-8, Hypotheses 4-4A, 4-5A).

What these variables have in common—the reason for their influencing behavior of the focal role—is the varying degrees of demand that they generate for controller involvement. The rationale was explained when formulating the hypotheses. The role sender's expectations may also be seen as influencing role behavior in this manner: the higher the role sender's expectations concerning a particular aspect of role behavior, the greater the demand for it.

Thus, it is possible to link situational variables to role behavior more directly than in the conceptual framework of role theory shown in Exhibit 7-1. The proposed modification is in Exhibit 7-2. According to this framework, situational factors not only influence role behavior indirectly via role sender expectations, as assumed in role theory (arrow 2), but also directly by generating a demand for role behavior (arrow 3) just as role sender expectations do (arrow 4). The translation of the demand for role behavior into actual role behavior is moderated by attributes of the person in the focal role and interpersonal factors, as in role theory (arrow 5).

Exhibit 7-1   Conceptual Framework of Role Theory

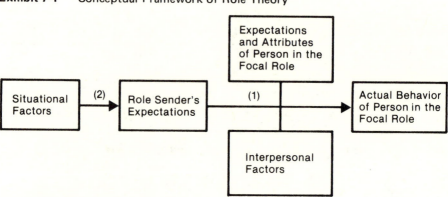

Daniel Katz and Robert L. Kahn, *The Social Psychology of Organizations,* 2nd ed. (New York: John Wiley, 1978), Chap. 7, p. 196.

Exhibit 7-2   Modified Conceptual Framework Based on Role Theory Concepts

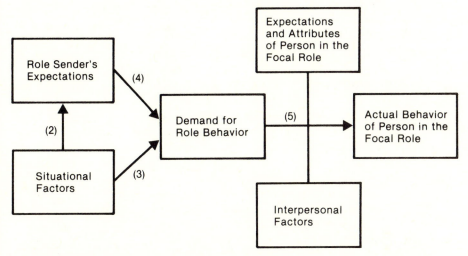

Daniel Katz and Robert L. Kahn, *The Social Psychology of Organizations,* 2nd ed. (New York: John Wiley, 1978), Chap. 7, and the findings of this book.

The question of how and why situational factors are related to role sender expectations has not received much research attention[10] and their independent and joint effects on role behavior have not been explored. Although these questions could not be addressed more adequately here using mulitvariate techniques, for reasons given in Chapter 3, the findings indicate that this is a rich arena for future research.

Implications for Contingency Theory of Organization

Chapter 6 focused on the degree of *typical* division controller involvement, which is an attribute of the company as a whole. These results are therefore relevant to macro-organization theory. In general, Chapter 6 indicates the influence of top executives' orientation, expectations, operating style, and management philosophy on the organizational attribute of interest—typical division controller involvement in the company. Other situational variables are of less importance (Exhibit 6-4).

Unfortunately, little previous macro-organizational research and theory have considered the influence of attributes of top management. This may be due partly to the difficulty of securing participation from those at the senior-most levels in a sufficient number of organizations to enable comparative analysis. (The low response rate obtained in this study and the reasons given by companies declining

[10] Katz and Kahn (1978), p. 208.

participation were mentioned in Chapter 3.) Or it may be that researchers have underestimated the importance of top executive choice in determining organizational characteristics.[11]

Although difficult to undertake, greater emphasis on attributes of top executives in future research on the behavior of organizations would yield three benefits. First, more integration between the macro and micro theories of organizational behavior would result, yielding rich dividends in the form of new synthesis. Second, such emphasis would generate systematic data on how external factors influence top executives' orientations, expectations, operating style, and management philosophy. Little work has been done in this area. Such understanding is needed given the important influence of management characteristics on the organization. Finally, since executives are concerned about what *ought* to be done, not just with descriptions of what generally tends to happen and why, their inclusion in future macro research may aid in the development of more prescriptive theory than is currently available. The implications of the study for such theory are now considered.

IMPLICATIONS FOR PRESCRIPTIVE ORGANIZATION THEORY

For a theory to be prescriptive, it must offer recommendations and suggestions, that is, prescriptions. To do so requires use of appropriate criteria for distinguishing between "better" and "worse" alternatives. What criteria are appropriate? The question is not strictly scientific in that it does not yield an answer that can be tested and found to be true or false, as Simon has pointed out:

> Factual propositions are statements about the observable world and the way in which it operates. In principle, factual propositions may be tested to determine whether they are *true* or *false*—whether what they say about the world actually occurs, or whether it does not. . . . [Administrative] decisions are something more than factual propositions. To be sure they are descriptive of a future state of affairs, and this description can be true or false in a strictly empirical sense; but they possess, in addition, an imperative quality—they select one future state of affairs in preference to another and direct behavior toward the chosen alternative. In short, they have an *ethical* as well as a factual content. . . . The question of whether [administrative] decisions can be correct or incorrect resolves itself, then, into a question of whether ethical terms like "ought," "good," and "preferable" have purely empirical meaning [all emphasis in the original].[12]

Drawing on the philosophy of science[13] for justification, Simon argues that ethical questions cannot be reduced to factual questions; hence, answers to these questions cannot, in an unqualified sense, be judged "correct" or "incorrect."

[11] Child (1972) and Lorsch and Allen (1973) are two notable exceptions.

[12] Simon (1945), p. 46.

[13] Simon bases his argument on "logical positivism."

This is why much social science research does not attempt to be prescriptive. Prescriptions are answers to "ethical" questions—in the sense that Simon uses the term—that many social scientists consider to be outside the realm of "science" because they cannot be verified as true or false. Although intended to be descriptive, such research is *in fact* used prescriptively or normatively, as Argyris has argued:

> The more the differentiation between descriptive and normative is examined, the fuzzier it becomes.... The author recently illustrated this consequence by the concepts of dissonance and attribution.... One can show empirically that the interpersonal world of most people in ongoing organizations is characterized by much more mistrust, conformity, and closedness than trust, individuality, and openness.... The predictions from dissonance or attribution theories can be readily confirmed in this Pattern A world. Thus, findings based on descriptive research will tend to opt for the status quo.

> If one creates a new pattern (Pattern B), which admittedly is very rare in the everyday world, where trust, openness, and individuality are able to predominate, the same predictions are no longer readily confirmable.

> If one replies that such behavior is rarely observed, we would agree and then ask for the systematic research to tell us how the behavior may be made more frequent. Twenty years ago no one had pole-vaulted higher than sixteen feet. Yet, no one took this as given. Today the sixteen-foot mark is broken continually because people focused on enhancing the potentiality of man. To take an example from the field of health, individuals with no cavities were rare, yet scholars of dental health conducted research with this goal in mind.[14]

Argyris's basic point is that, because descriptive research is in fact used normatively, it ends up reinforcing the status quo unless explicit attention is paid to normative factors in conducting research. He and others have argued that such attention not only has the potential for improving practice but also for facilitating the development of better theory; that is, scholars can learn by trying to put their theories into practice.[15] In agreement, it might be added that since the criteria chosen for normative or prescriptive research cannot be judged correct or incorrect in a scientific sense—they are based on answers to ethical questions—it is important to be specific about what criteria are used, and why, so that others can judge their appropriateness.

The sections following contain a description of the criteria that may be considered appropriate for examining the questions of staff effectiveness and the broader question of organizational effectiveness.

[14] Argyris (1973), p. 160.
[15] Argyris and Schon (1974); Susman and Evered (1978).

**A Conceptual Framework
for Examining Staff Effectiveness**

According to the traditional literature on line and staff, the relevant criteria for judging better and worse staff work, that is, staff effectiveness, are the quality of information, analysis, and advice given to line management. However, an analysis of this literature and more recent work, undertaken in Chapter 1, as well as the findings documented in the book, indicate that the degree of staff involvement in business decision making may be a more relevant criterion by which to judge staff effectiveness. The degree of importance of this criterion varies according to the situation. Where the general manager and operating executives are themselves trained in the staff area in question, the importance of staff involvement is less than it is in other cases. Similarly, where the nature of the business or environment makes contribution in the staff area in question particularly critical, the importance of staff involvement is greater than in other cases. In general, because of increasing size and complexity of the modern corporation, the importance of staff involvement is likely to increase in the future.

Another effectiveness criterion is also important when the staff role in question has some responsibility for monitoring the decisions and actions of affiliated management. Just as public concern over the accuracy of financial reporting and the integrity of internal control led to the formation of the Securities and Exchange Commission in 1933 and resulted in increased emphasis on the controller's custodial and monitoring responsibility,[16] the mounting external pressures of litigation and regulation on the modern corporation make the monitoring responsibility more important for other staff roles today, for example, personnel, legal, product design, quality assurance.

The greater the external pressure on the corporation in a particular area of staff work, the greater the importance of staff independence in that area. The extent to which executives at high levels in the organization have confidence in the integrity and good judgment of those on lower levels are also important: the greater the confidence, the lower the importance of staff independence. Thus, staff effectiveness may be judged by the extent to which the degree of actual staff involvement and independence are consistent with their degree of importance in light of the situation.

A conceptual scheme depicting major factors influencing the degree of importance of staff involvement and independence are shown in Exhibit 7-3. Factors influencing the degree of actual staff involvement are shown in Exhibit 7-2. Although not examined in this study, the scheme in Exhibit 7-2 seems applicable to staff independence as well, since this is one aspect of role behavior (staff involvement being the other). What remains to be mentioned is the difficulty of actually achieving high degrees of both involvement and independence as indicated by the negative sign connecting the two in Exhibit 7-3. It appears that the key to overcoming the apparent dilemma lies in having staff with certain personal qualities

---

[16] Jackson (1949); Bradshaw and Hull (1950).

Exhibit 7-3 Conceptual Framework for Study of Staff Effectiveness

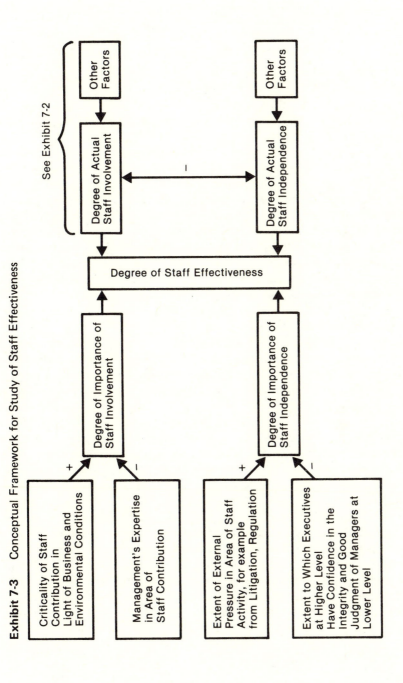

and interpersonal and other skills described in the next chapter under the section on development of strong controllers. The next section contains a brief discussion of the implications of the study for the question of organizational effectiveness.

A New Conceptualization
of Organizational Effectiveness

The question of staff effectiveness is one aspect of the broader question of organizational effectiveness. Various criteria have been used in previous research on the latter question. A recent review of the literature[17] covering 17 models of organizational effectiveness yielded 14 evaluation criteria. Future work in this area would be facilitated if researchers can agree on the dimensions of central importance, as pointed out in a recent critique: "The theoretical underpinnings of the concept of organizational effectiveness have not been delineated and there is little agreement about . . . the focal element of effectiveness. Indeed, pertinent research and debate show little cumulative character and even less theoretical direction."[18]

Although this study was not focused on the question of organizational effectiveness, a criterion that captures some of the dimensions of effectiveness found to be important in this and earlier work is being suggested.

Criterion of Effectiveness
An important measure of degree of individual or organizational effectiveness is the extent to which the individual or organization has simultaneously achieved desirable states that appear to be mutually inconsistent or contradictory, that is, the extent to which apparent dilemmas or tensions have been overcome.

The basis for this criterion is the notion of competitive advantage. If an individual or an organization has overcome an apparent dilemma or contradiction, it has done what relevant others find difficult to do. To the extent that both "horns" of the apparent dilemma are desirable, the individual or organization is at an advantage over relevant others. The apparent tensions found in this study are those of independence versus involvement and risk taking versus control (Chapter 2). Those found in earlier work are differentiation versus integration,[19] efficiency versus adaptability,[20] and concern with production versus concern with people.[21]

Consider the suggested criterion of effectiveness in light of the earlier discussion on descriptive versus prescriptive theory. In traditional social science research, a random sample of individuals or organizations would be studied and a negative association for each pair of variables cited would be observed. The implications

[17] Steers (1975), p. 549.
[18] Pennings (1977), p. 538.
[19] Lawrence and Lorsch (1967).
[20] Georgopoulous and Tannenbaum (1957); Mott (1972); Lawrence (1980).
[21] Blake and Mouton (1964).

would be that a high value for one of the variables in each pair is generally associated with a low value for the other. If left at that, students and practitioners might assume that the relationships govern and, believing this, behave on that basis.

Prescriptive research would attempt to understand why some individuals and organizations defy these relationships. Rather than viewing these cases as "outliers" to be deleted from further analysis, they would be examined further to discover why they have the characteristics not generally observed. The associated consequences would also be explored. To the extent that these cases represent an "improvement" over the relationships generally obtained, such research provides guidance for improved practice. For instance, the work for Lawrence and Lorsch[22] indicates how some organizations are able to achieve higher degrees of both differentiation *and* integration even though in general a high degree of one is associated with a low degree of the other. The keys to overcoming the dilemma are a variety of integrating mechanisms, including reliance on confrontation as the primary mode of conflict resolution.

In the concluding section of this chapter questions are raised about some trends and relationships that were uncovered. The available evidence is scanty because these relationships were not being investigated; rather, they emerged from the data and analysis. They are highlighted in the hope that they will be addressed in future work.

IMPORTANT QUESTIONS
THAT REMAIN UNANSWERED

The "Substitution Effect"

In companies in which the chief executive officer had a financial background, the corporate controller was not actively involved in business decisions (Hypothesis 4-4 in Chapter 4). Similarly, division managers with financial backgrounds invariably had division controllers who were not actively involved in business decisions. It is not known if similar patterns exist in other staff areas, but they could be expected if the explanation given earlier is valid. This finding raises an important issue concerning the development of staff working with general managers who are trained in the area of the staff's expertise.

While the lack of staff contribution under these conditions may be of little concern from the standpoint of effective decision making, because the general manager "substitutes" for the staff and thus brings the necessary specialist judgment and expertise to bear when business decisions are made, the consequences for staff development are unclear. To the extent that individuals learn by "seeing" others in action, a person may learn a great deal by association with another of his or her own particular functional background carrying out general management responsibilities. However, to the extent that one learns by "doing," persons in staff positions not actively involved are denied the experience and learning that comes from

[22] Lawrence and Lorsch (1967).

placing one's analysis and judgment "on the line"—from recommending action and challenging the plans and actions of others, including the boss.

An analogous phenomenon with similar effects for management development is the following.

The "Egomaniacs"

Executives in the two "pattern 1" companies described the present or former chief executive officer as an "egotistical" person who was responsible for the company's "weak" managers (see Chapter 2). Four other general managers in this study were described similarly by colleagues and/or subordinates and were also blamed for developing "weak" managers.

Managers use the terms "strong" and "weak" to refer to a variety of attributes—technical competence, maturity, judgment, and so on—depending on the context of the discussion. What was meant by "weak" in the present context seemed to refer to managers who were not actively involved in the decision-making process (in the sense of recommending action and challenging colleagues and their boss) because the latter's ego would not permit it. The development of these managers probably suffered because they were denied the opportunity for learning that comes from more active involvement.

Both the "substitution effect" and the "egomaniacs" have an important influence on management development and deserve some attention in future research.

The "Inbreeding" Phenomenon

The phenomenon of "inbreeding" refers to the finding of this study that, in companies in which the chief executive officer has a financial background, the percentage of senior corporate executives with financial backgrounds is *significantly* greater than in other companies (see Exhibit 4-5 in Chapter 4). Again, it is not known if the finding generalizes to other functional specialties, that is, if chief executive officers in general tend to surround themselves with a large proportion of senior executives of like background, but it raises some important questions.

Why does this occur? Is it because an executive feels more comfortable when surrounded by others of similar background? What are the implications for the management "culture" at the top? One interpretation of the "substitution effect" just described is that a general manager tends to dominate a subordinate of similar background. If this is the case, the implications for the phenomenon of inbreeding are worthy of attention. Chief executive officers that surround themselves with executives of similar background may result in more domineering chief executive officers. Is this in the best interest of the corporation?

Inbreeding could be dysfunctional because of insufficient attention to other specialist viewpoints. Or, somewhat counterintuitively, inbreeding may be dysfunctional because of *excessive* emphasis on other specialist viewpoints as suggested by one corporate controller who reviewed the working draft of this book: "The chief executive officer becomes overinfluenced by the mystique of the other disciplines and may assume that some items are self-proven."

Balance of Risk Taking and Control

As the four basic "patterns" of risk taking and control indicate (Chapter 2), there are benefits to be derived from increased risk taking and control. But there is tension in the relationship between them: several companies had high degrees of one or the other; few had both. The appropriate balance between risk taking and control is worthy of further examination.

A comparison of the case histories of company 14 (in the text) and company 15 (in the Case Appendix) of Chapter 2 is instructive. Both companies compete in the same basic industry—foods—but company 14 seems to have achieved a better balance between risk taking and control. How is this done? Management balance at the top and the management culture appear to be two important ways.

Company 14 has a more balanced perspective at the top. The chief executive officer, the chief operating officer, and the chief financial officer had all held positions in a variety of functional disciplines. In contrast, the chief executive officer at company 15 had a predominantly financial background and is surrounded by a large proportion of senior corporate executives who also have financial backgrounds. The second important distinction is the difference in the management culture of the two companies. Although a "mushy" concept, a reading of the brief case histories of the two companies in Chapter 2 leaves one with the distinct impression that these are two very different managerial worlds in which to live. Perhaps the phrase "creative tension and trust" best describes the management culture at company 14. The phrase "risk aversion and chief executive officer's domination" might characterize the management culture at company 15. While these differences exist, it is not known how exactly they influence the balance of risk taking and control or how the right balance may be achieved.

The next chapter presents some indication of how the dilemma of controller involvement versus controller independence may be overcome. Other implications of this study for practical affairs are also discussed.

chapter 8

Implications for Practical Affairs

In both Parts I and II of this book the discussion was descriptive rather than prescriptive. The emphasis was on what tends to happen in the companies studied, not on what these and other companies ought to do about controller involvement and related matters. This chapter deals with the latter subject by discussing the implications of the research for practical affairs.

Since the practitioner is centrally concerned with improved performance, the material in Part I, particularly the findings on controller involvement and company performance in Chapter 2, are relied on in this discussion. What the models developed in Part II provide is an understanding of how various contextual factors influence the degree of controller involvement. Together, these factors may be seen as determining the constraints and opportunities for controller involvement; that is, they influence the "context" for controller involvement. Depending on the particular vantage point of the reader (that is, corporate management versus division management, controller versus general manager), one or more of these contextual factors are amenable to change, thus altering the constraints or opportunities for controller involvement. Whatever the particular context, however, it is also possible to increase the level of involvement on the basis of personal motivation, initiative, and the acquisition of certain skills to be described later.

Four major topics are covered in this chapter. First, because the division controller has two seemingly contradictory responsibilities—involvement in business decisions and independence from management—what should the division controller's role emphasize? Is it better to assign the two responsibilities to different individuals? Second, what can a company do to develop strong controllers—those who can remain actively involved in business decisions while retaining a sense of objectivity and independence from affiliated management? Third, what should the role of the corporate controller be? Should the board of directors be more actively involved in determining this role? The recent public disclosures concerning corporate kickbacks, illegal payments, and financial mismanagement make this an important practical question worthy of objective examination. Finally, because other staff positions, such as personnel and legal, are increasingly experiencing the dual pressures of the controller's role, what are the implications for other staff roles in management?

WHAT SHOULD THE ROLE
OF THE DIVISION CONTROLLER BE?

An examination of staff roles in general and that of the controller in particular, undertaken in Part I, indicates why active controller involvement is important. Essentially, because of increasing organizational size and complexity, it is in the corporation's best interest to ensure that specialist knowledge and expertise are brought to bear when business decisions are made. This requires that the staff executives in question—the controller in this case—be actively involved in the business decision-making process. Although unable to quantify its magnitude, most managers in this study recognized the important contributions that the controller can make in the following areas of management activity: planning and control of receivables, inventories, operating expenses, and capital expenditures; financial analysis; and management of taxes.

In addition to the responsibility for making these contributions, requiring active involvement in business decisions, the controller is also responsible for the accuracy of financial reporting and for the integrity of internal control (see Exhibit 1-1 and items 1 and 2 in the related summary in Chapter 1). These last two responsibilities, custodial and monitoring in nature and requiring a degree of independence from management, are also of increasing importance.

In the wake of several public disclosures concerning corporate kickbacks and other illegal payments, for instance, the U.S. Congress in 1977 passed the Foreign Corrupt Practices Act, which is not limited to matters either foreign or corrupt. It covers all transactions, and to comply with the provisions of the law an adequate system of internal controls must be maintained. Companies and their executives are subject to civil and criminal liability if they do not comply. In response to these concerns, most large corporations today have a strong internal audit staff at headquarters, who periodically visit the field locations. However, this group cannot offer the *continuous* vigilance that the local controller can. Neither do corporate auditors typically have the depth of knowledge about local systems, people, and practices to be able to detect subtle misrepresentations or inadequacies. Thus, the corporation must rely on the local controller to be an effective local guardian. To do so, the local controller's independence must be ensured.

Since the controller's responsibilities for financial reporting and internal control, calling for controller independence from management, and the responsibility for management service, requiring active involvement in business decisions, both are of considerable importance, the following critical question arises: Are these responsibilities compatible? Can the controller wear these two hats effectively—one that of an umpire or police officer, the other that of a helper or counsellor?

Some have argued that the answer is no: "The helping role and the role of policeman are absolutely incompatible roles. To place an individual in the latter is to destroy the possibility of his occupying the former one successfully."[1]

This book both supports and challenges this position. While both controllers and other managers generally *perceived* the requirement for controller involvement to be somewhat at odds with the requirement for controller independence, "strong" controllers were identified as those able to overcome the perceived contradiction and become actively involved in business decisions while retaining objectivity and independence. Performance of one responsibility may be perceived as making the performance of the other responsibility more difficult—and may in fact do so for some individuals—but others can overcome this dilemma.

Because the controller's responsibilities for financial reporting and internal control may be somewhat inconsistent with the management service responsibility, but not necessarily so, what should the role of the division controller be? Four possibilities exist: (1) place high emphasis on the controller's management service responsibility but low emphasis on the financial reporting and internal control responsibilities, (2) place high emphasis on the controller's financial reporting and internal control responsibilities but low emphasis on the management service responsibility, (3) split up the division controller's role and assign each responsibility to a different individual in order to place high emphasis on both responsibilities, and (4) retain the management service and the financial reporting and internal control responsibilities with one individual but place high emphasis on both.[2]

Each of these possibilities may be viewed as a "prototype"of what the role of the division controller should be. Since each of these ideal types has certain potential benefits and costs associated with it, what is needed is a method for determining which type of role is best suited for a given company. The pros and cons of each role type are discussed first; a procedure that management can use in choosing the type best suited to its needs is suggested next.

Four Types of Role for Division Controllers

The potential benefits and costs associated with each of the four role types are summarized in Exhibit 8-1.

If primary emphasis is placed on the controller's management service responsibility (involved controller), the desired behavior is for the controller to actively

[1] McGregor (1960), p. 169.

[2] The placing of a low emphasis on both the major controller responsibilities is a fifth possibility, but one that is unlikely to be sought in practice for reasons given in the foregoing discussion. If it is deemed appropriate, a controller who is technically competent would be adequate. No special personal characteristics, or interpersonal or other skills demanded of the other role types, to be discussed later in this chapter, would be required.

participate in the business decision-making process. The potential benefits are the contributions that result in the control of receivables, inventories, operating expenses, and capital expenditures, as well as other contributions that result because appropriate financial analysis and expertise are brought to bear when business decisions are made. The potential costs, however, are the stifling of management creativity and initiative that may result from active controller involvement, as indicated in Chapter 2, and the limited assurance of adequate financial reporting and internal control.

If primary emphasis is placed on the controller's financial reporting and internal control responsibilities (independent controller), the desired behavior is for the controller to retain objectivity and independence in dealing with affiliated management. The potential benefits are greater assurance concerning the accuracy of financial reporting and the integrity of internal control. Again, there are potential costs. The controller's contribution to business decisions is limited in this case. Also, because the primary emphasis is on the custodial and monitoring responsibilities, the controller is in danger of being viewed by local management as an "outsider" if not a "corporate spy." To that extent, he or she may be denied access to sensitive information by local management whenever possible, making it difficult to put an early stop to ill-conceived courses of action; that is, if the controller is not privy to all sensitive management deliberations in progress, he or she may not have the opportunity to prevent ill-advised or illegal matters from receiving consideration. If so, the controller can only check compliance with corporate policy and procedures *after* the relevant decisions and actions have already been taken. The resulting control may be characterized as "after-the-fact," or reactive, control rather than "before-the-fact," or anticipatory, control.

There are two ways in which high emphasis may be placed on the controller's financial reporting and internal control *and* management service responsibilities. The first of these (split controller) is to split the division controller's role and assign each major responsibility to a different individual. The potential benefits are the undivided attention that each of the major responsibilities now receives. There are four potential costs, however.

First, to the extent that the same information and analysis are the basis for the performance of the financial reporting, internal control, and management service responsibilities, this approach is inefficient because of the duplication of effort and resources involved. Second, it weakens the coordination between various phases of the same basic function because a single executive is not in overall charge of all the controllership responsibilities. Third, the person assigned the financial reporting and internal control responsibilities ("external" controller) stands to be isolated from division management in much the same way as the independent controller, thus making possible after-the-fact control rather than before-the-fact control. While the person assigned the management services responsibility ("internal" controller) may be privy to all sensitive management information and deliberations in progress, his or her continued effectiveness may depend on not divulging this knowledge to the "external" counterpart. Finally, the "internal" controller's active involvement in business decisions could stifle management creativity and initiative, as in the case of the involved controller.

Exhibit 8-1 Potential Benefits and Costs of Four Types of Roles for Division Controllers

Role Type[a]	Division Controller's Role	Required Behavior for Division Controller	Potential Benefits	Potential Costs
Involved Controller	Assign high emphasis to the controller's management service responsibility and low emphasis to the financial reporting and internal control responsibilities	Remain actively involved in division business decisions	Contribution to divisional business decisions	Stifling of management creativity and initiative Limited assurance of accurate financial reporting and adequate internal control ("after-the-fact" control)
Independent Controller	Assign high emphasis to the controller's financial reporting and internal control responsibilities and low emphasis to the management service responsibilities	Retain objectivity and independence from division management	Assurance of accurate financial reporting and adequate internal control ("after-the-fact" control)	Controller viewed as "outsider," making "before-the-fact" control difficult to achieve Limited contribution to divisional business decisions
Split Controller	Split the division controller's role and assign the management service and financial reporting and internal control	The controller assigned the management service responsibility to remain actively involved in division business decisions	Contributions to divisional business decisions Assurance of accurate financial	Duplication of effort and resources Weakening of coordination between two

Exhibit 8-1 (continued)

Role Type[a]	Division Controller's Role	Required Behavior for Division Controller	Potential Benefits	Potential Costs
	responsibilities to different individuals, placing high emphasis on both responsibilites	The controller assigned the financial control and internal audit responsibilities to retain a sense of objectivity and independence from division management	reporting and adequate internal control	phases of the same function "Before-the-fact" control difficult to achieve "Stifling" of management creativity and initiative
Stong Controller	Assign both management service and financial reporting and internal control responsibilities to one individual and place high emphasis on both responsibilities	Remain actively involved in division business decisions while retaining objectivity and independence from division management	Contributions to divisional business decisions Assurance of accurate financial reporting and adequate internal control "Before-the fact," or anticipatory, control	Selection, training, and development of "strong" division controllers (that is, those who have the strength of character and the interpersonal and other skills needed to achieve both high involvement *and* high independence) Stifling of management creativity and initiative

[a]A fifth role type (low emphasis on management service responsibility and low emphasis on the financial control and internal reporting responsibilities) places no special demands on the controller and is not considered here. A controller who is competent in a technical sense would suffice; no special personal characteristics and interpersonal or other skills demanded of the other role types, as discussed later in this chapter, would be required.

Finally, both the major controller responsibilities may be retained with one individual but high emphasis placed on both (strong controller). The desired behavior is for the controller to remain actively involved in the local business decision-making process while retaining a sense of objectivity and independence from affiliated management. There are three potential benefits if controllers operate in this way. First, there are the controller contributions that result because of active participation in business decision making. Second, there is the assurance of valid financial reporting and adequate internal control. Finally, because the controller is actively involved in the business decision-making process, he or she has access to all sensitive management information and deliberations in progress. As such, he or she has the opportunity to put an early stop to ill-conceived, ill-advised, or illegal decisions and courses of action being contemplated. The result is "before-the-fact" control not obtained with the other role types discussed previously. More responsive control is thus possible when a company has controllers who can retain a sense of objectivity and independence while remaining actively involved in the business decision-making process.

The strong controller role has its costs also. It demands of the controller greater interpersonal and other skills than those required under the other role types. The effort required to select, train, and develop such controllers is outlined later.

Since each role type has certain potential costs and benefits, management needs to make a trade-off in light of the company's situation and determine which type is best suited to its own particular situation. A procedure for making this determination is now presented.

Criteria for Determining the Role of Division Controller

Because the controller's responsibilities are but one part of the management task, the choice of an appropriate role for the controller cannot be made in isolation. The relationship of the controller's role to other management roles must be considered. Both assessments of the latter roles as currently performed as well as questions about what these roles should be are relevant. Because this book does not examine all management roles, current assessments of how other roles are performed are used as a basis for determining what the controller's role should be. Changes in the other management roles would require corresponding changes in the role of the controller.

Suggested criteria for determining what the division controller's role should be are summarized in Exhibit 8-2. Two questions must be asked in determining the emphasis that should be placed on the controller's management service responsibility. First, what are the benefits of the controller's potential contribution in local business decisions in relation to the potential costs of stifled management creativity and initiative that may result? On the one hand, as was mentioned, controller involvement can lead to contributions in the control of receivables, inventories, operating expenses, and capital expenditures as well as the other benefits that

Exhibit 8-2   Criteria for Determining Role
of Division Controller

Required Emphasis on the Division Controller's Management Service Responsibility
(higher scores argue for greater emphasis)

---

1. Net benefits from the division controller's potential contribution to business decisions in relation to the potential costs of stifled management creativity and initiative

1	2	3	4	5
Limited		Moderate		Considerable

2. Division management's expertise in the areas of division controller's potential contribution

5	4	3	2	1
Limited		Moderate		Considerable

Required Emphasis on the Division Controller's Financial Reporting
and Internal Control Responsibilities
(higher scores argue for greater emphasis)

---

1. Corporate concern about the accuracy of financial reporting and the adequacy of internal control

1	2	3	4	5
Limited		Moderate		Considerable

2. Corporate confidence in the integrity and good judgment of division management

5	4	3	2	1
Limited		Moderate		Considerable

---

accrue because financial analysis and expertise are brought to bear when business decisions are made. On the other hand, as indicated in Chapter 2, active controller involvement has the potential for stifling management creativity and initiative. Operating executives may view such involvement as an "infringement" on their areas of authority and responsibility.

As the increasing experience with matrix organizations indicates, however, management approaches based on the concept of shared authority and responsibility work where managers have the interpersonal skills needed to handle the increased ambiguity.[3] Also, as two recent works indicate, power—not mere formal authority—is needed for increased managerial effectiveness.[4] Such management

[3] Davis and Lawrence (1977).

[4] Kotter (1977) argues that power is needed for managerial effectiveness because formal authority is insufficient for managing the dependencies inherent in managerial work, as McGregor (1960) pointed out. Making essentially the same argument, Kanter (1979) discusses three roles in which greater power is particularly needed: first-line supervisors, staff professionals, and chief executive officers.

approaches require greater interpersonal and other skills than are needed when formal authority is relied on as the only source of influence.

Thus, to what extent active controller involvement in business decisions actually dampens management creativity and initiative depends on what the prevailing managerial approach is. If managers emphasize formal authority in influencing others' behavior, they are likely to experience the controller's involvement as a threat to their prerogatives. Where the role of formal authority in organizational life is downplayed, the actual danger of stifled managerial creativity and initiative is likely to be far less. What is needed, therefore, is an assessment of the actual risks and benefits of active controller involvement in light of the prevailing environmental, business, and management conditions. The greater the net benefits, the higher the required emphasis on the controller's management service responsibility.

The second important criterion to consider is, to what extent do other members of local management have expertise in the areas in which the controller can potentially contribute? The career paths in some companies are such that several operating executives have prior experience in finance or control. In other companies, there are few, if any, such executives in operating management. To the extent that other managers have expertise in the areas in which the controller can make a special contribution, they themselves bring the necessary financial knowledge and skill to bear when business decisions are made. Since they effectively substitute for the controller, the latter's contribution is of less importance. Thus, the greater the local management's expertise in the controller's areas of contribution, the lower the required emphasis on the controller's management service responsibility.

As far as the controller's other major responsibilities are concerned, the following two criteria are important. First, what is the extent of the corporate concern about the accuracy of financial reporting and the adequacy of internal control? There will be considerable corporate concern about the performance of these controller responsibilities if there have been instances of "blowups," that is, large and *unanticipated* write-offs of inventory and receivables in one or more operating units, or if there have been recent disclosures of financial irresponsibility, or if the divisions have been frequently unable to meet corporate requests for reliable, timely information. If the corporation is not plagued by such unpleasant "surprises," corporate concern about the controller's financial reporting and internal control responsibilities may be limited. The greater the corporate concern in these areas, the higher the required emphasis on these controller responsibilities.

Second, what is the level of trust and confidence that corporate executives have in the integrity and good judgment of the division managers? Such confidence would be low where there have been recent unpleasant surprises of the type just described. Confidence may be low even if such surprises have not recently occurred simply because the corporate or division managers are relatively new to the company and have not yet developed the necessary interpersonal trust or because the personalities involved find it difficult to develop such trust.[5] The greater the corporate confidence in the integrity and good judgment of division management,

---

[5] Lawler (1976), p. 1286.

the lower the required emphasis on the controller's financial reporting and internal control responsibilities.

An assessment of its own situation using the criteria summarized in Exhibit 8-2 provides corporate management with a basis for determining the emphasis to be placed on the division controller's two major responsibilities. If the management service responsibility deserves high emphasis and the financial reporting and internal control responsibilities low emphasis, the involved controller role is indicated (see Exhibit 8-1). If the opposite is true, the independent controller role is recommended. If both the management service and financial reporting and internal control responsibilities deserve high emphasis, management needs to carefully consider the trade-offs involved in determining whether the split controller or the strong controller role is better suited to its own situation.[6]

The strong controller role offers superior control, that is, "before-the-fact," or anticipatory, control rather than "after-the-fact," or reactive, control and does not have the other potential costs associated with the split controller role, but it is more difficult to implement. It requires that controllers have the strength of character and the interpersonal and other skills needed to overcome the difficulty of achieving high degrees of both involvement *and* independence. A company cannot implement this approach overnight. The behaviors and skills required are to some extent counterintuitive and are not typically addressed in the education and training of controllers. Although the necessary talent may not be readily available on the market, companies can facilitate the development of individuals with the required skills and behavior, as described later in this chapter.

Changing the Role of Division Controller

A comparison of the desired role for the company's division controllers as determined by the procedure in the preceding section and the actual role as currently performed would indicate what changes, if any, are needed. If greater controller emphasis on the management service responsibilities is sought, the desired behavior change is for the division controllers to participate more actively in the business decision-making process. The material in Part II indicates how this may be facilitated. If greater controller emphasis on the financial reporting and internal control responsibilities is needed, the desired behavior change is for the division controllers to retain greater objectivity and independence when dealing with division management. While this book does not focus on controller independence, it does suggest some approaches to be described shortly that may be used by those seeking to increase it.

The means by which corporate management can influence the degree of division controller involvement are shown in Exhibit 6-4. One or more of these avenues may be relied on to alter division controller involvement depending on preference and

[6] If both major responsibilities require low emphasis, an unlikely possibility in today's business environment, see footnote 2.

assessment of the situation. The corporate controller can influence the degree of division controller involvement in two important ways: by emphasizing the service role in dealings with division management and by providing a *sustained* emphasis on the development of controllership personnel within the company. Each of these possibilities is considered now.

Corporate controllers who emphasize the service role in dealings with division managment appear to enhance the degree of division controller involvement by signaling the importance of the service role to both division controllers and division managers. Also, because corporate controllers who emphasize the service role also tend to be themselves actively involved in business decisions at corporate head-quarters (Hypothesis 6-11), they are more likely to have an in-depth understanding of business issues and problems and thus more apt to be perceived by division management as having greater credibility. As a result, they probably have greater leverage over division management, giving them a better chance of influencing division controller involvement.

As for personnel development, the data indicate that a *sustained* emphasis is needed before the efforts bear fruit (compare Hypotheses 6-12 and 6-13). It takes time to select, train, and develop controllers with the necessary qualities and skills. The specifics of such development are detailed in the next section of this chapter.

Corporate management can signal the desired behavior change, that is, greater division controller involvement in business decisions, in a variety of ways. One is to ensure that the corporate controller serves as a "role model" for the companies division controllers, that is, is himself or herself actively involved in business deci-sion making. Greater corporate controller involvement may be induced by altering one or more of the contextual factors in Exhibit 4-7; the setting of high expecta-tions regarding his or her involvement is probably the most feasible avenue available in this regard. If the current corporate controller is unwilling or unable to perform the needed role, the appointment of a replacement who can do so should be con-sidered. This was the approach commonly taken by the companies in this study that had successfully increased the level of division controller involvement.

Other signals are available to corporate management seeking greater involvement from the company's division controllers. One is for the chief executive officer to ask the corporate controller to "talk about the company's controllers" at a senior management meeting, as was done in one company studied. The following ques-tions were asked: "How many of our controllers are high flyers? Dead wood? What are we doing to help both groups? Are we moving people around?" In another com-pany, controllers who had not previously participated in the divisional management bonus plan were included "in recognition of their important contribution to the company." In a third, division management was asked to prepare job descriptions for their controllers that were then used as a basis for clarifying corporate expecta-tions.

Although this book is not focused on controller independence, it does point to two basic approaches taken by those companies examined that were attempting to increase the level of division controller independence. One approach was to switch reporting relationships—from the common arrangement, in which division controllers report directly to the division general managers with a technical ("dotted line") responsibility to the corporate controller, to an arrangement in which division controllers report directly (on a "solid line") to the corporate controller. Two of the 24 companies in this study (8 percent) had done this within the previous three years to signal heightened corporate concern about the lack of controller independence. In an earlier survey of 129 *Fortune* "1000" companies,[7] 10 of the surveyed companies (8 percent of the 129) had adopted this arrangement within three years prior to the survey.

Another approach used to address heightened corporate concern about lack of controller independence is to split the division controller's role by assigning the management service responsibility to one individual and the financial reporting and internal control responsibilities to another. Two companies in this study had adopted such an arrangement. The executive formally designated as "division controller" was assigned the financial reporting and internal control functions; another divisional executive performed the management service function. Significantly, both were oil companies. (A third oil company in the study hadn't done so.) These companies are required to comply with special rules and regulations concerning the accounting and reporting of petroleum production, inventory, and distribution. Management in these companies is also particularly sensitive about their public image following the oil embargo of 1973 and the subsequent public debate concerning whether or not the oil companies should be split up to increase competition and limit "excess" profit. In these companies, management is especially concerned about avoiding additional adverse publicity stemming from inaccurate reporting or inadequate control.

Changes in division controller reporting relationships or the more radical approach of actually splitting up the division controller's role may be viable approaches to increasing controller independence under certain circumstances, but the associated drawbacks make these approaches unattractive for other companies. The problems of switching to "solid line" reporting between the corporate and division controllers have been discussed elsewhere.[8] Essentially, this organizational arrangement is difficult to implement, and once implemented, there is the potential danger that the division controller may be isolated from local management. The disadvantages of splitting the controller's role were discussed earlier in this chapter.

Ultimately, division controller independence is assured by selecting individuals with strength of character and an independence of mind and by training and developing them so they have the requisite knowledge and skill to appropriately discharge this important responsibility. Guidelines for accomplishing this are now presented along with those for the achievement of high controller involvement.

---

[7] Sathe (1978b).
[8] Sathe (1978a, 1978b).

DEVELOPING STRONG DIVISION CONTROLLERS

As defined previously, "strong" controllers are those who are able to remain actively involved in the business decision-making process while retaining a sense of objectivity and independence in dealings with affiliated management. Although this is difficult to do, corporate management can facilitate such accomplishment by appropriately "managing the context," that is, by altering the contextual variables as just discussed to create a culture that encourages both high controller involvement and high controller independence. Success also depends on whether or not the company has individuals with the personal qualities and the technical and interpersonal skills needed to perform this difficult role. As one European corporate controller who reviewed the working draft of this book pointed out, "The profile required of a strong controller is so demanding that finding such a person would be difficult. A reduction of the required skills is desirable."

This comment partly reflects continental differences: unlike their counterparts in the United States, controllers in Europe are not always a part of the management team. Nonetheless, persons with the necessary qualities and skills are not readily available in the United States either. A company seeking strong controllers thus has two basic choices. It can either recruit individuals from corporations with a reputation for having strong controllers,[9] or it can "grow its own" strong controllers. The former approach must address the problem of assimilating the new "breed" into the existing organization. The latter technique takes time to bear fruit—three to five years is a conservative estimate based on the experience of companies that have successfully taken this approach. In either case, a substantial commitment of resources is needed to attract, retain, and develop the necessary strength.

Companies that are unable or unwilling to make such a commitment should reassess their own situation using Exhibit 8-2 to determine if one of the other three role types shown in Exhibit 8-1 (involved, independent, or split controller) is acceptable. These roles demand less of the incumbents, but each has its own disadvantages which the company must either live with or overcome by other means.

Although much has been written about the education and training of controllers,[10] the specific qualities and skills required of strong controllers have not been clearly defined or adequately emphasized. What are mentioned to be important attributes for controllers are typically couched in phrases such as "people skills" or "communication skills," which convey limited meaning about the specific skills required and how they may be acquired.

Detailed guidelines for those interested in the development of strong controllers are presented now. Since the achievement of both high controller involvement and high controller independence is addressed, the guidelines are comprehensive and cover aspects important in the effective performances of the other controller roles

---

[9] According to one account in the business press, "Such well-known controller training grounds as Xerox, GM, Ford, ITT, and General Electric are often raided by other corporations for new personnel." (*Business Week,* August 15, 1977, p. 95).

[10] Jannell and Kinnunen (1980); Stoddard (1978); and Stoughton (1978) are recent examples.

Exhibit 8-3   Characteristics of Strong Controllers

Characteristic Number	Description of Characteristic	Specific Attributes and Behaviors
	Personal Qualities	
1.	Personal energy and motivation	Is a doer. Is aware of everything going on. Takes initiative.
2.	Personal integrity and professional commitment	Is unbiased source of information. Doesn't try to bluff ("I don't know, but I'll find out"). Is the conscience of the division. Is not a "yes man." Is candid.
	Technical Competence	
3.	Accounting knowledge	Technical ability is not in question.
4.	Analytical skill	Determines not only what happened but also why something happened. Is good at arranging and rearranging numbers. Is able to spot trends before they become a reality. Is able to dig below the numbers.
	Business Judgment	
5.	Understanding of what management needs to run the business effectively	Is a businessperson. Has good business judgment. Is familiar with other parts of the division. Understands the division's business. Anticipates future business problems. Recommends action to deal with future business problems. Keeps an eye on the whole business. Is not always concerned about not spending.
	Communication Skills	
6.	Ability to judge what is important to management and make recommendations	Does not think only of financial control. Is able to summarize quickly and accurately.

Exhibit 8-3   (continued)

Characteristic Number	Description of Characteristic	Specific Attributes and Behaviors
		Mentally makes the same decisions as the division general manager.
		Provides management with information even before it realizes the need for it.
		Thinks the way the division manager thinks.
		Quickly grasps information of real concern to management.
		Is willing to estimate.
		Is able to judge the degree of accuracy needed.
		Does not emphasize accuracy as an end in itself.
		Does not get lost in allocating costs.
		Speaks the language used by management.
		Keeps the audience in mind.
		Is able to come to grips with facts and make recommendations.

Interpersonal Skills

Characteristic Number	Description of Characteristic	Specific Attributes and Behaviors
7.	Building relationships and developing influence	Gets along with everyone.
		Is accepted by all functional areas.
		Is part of the management team.
		Is management's trusted counselor.
		Is flexible in meeting management's demands.
		Is the general manager's alter ego.
		Is a sounding board for management when sensitive issues are discussed.
		Opens up communications.
		Is respected by management.
		Is trusted by management.
		Builds trust.
8.	Ability to challenge management constructively	Asks the right questions.
		Thinks about the impact of numbers.

Exhibit 8-3 (continued)

Characteristic Number	Description of Characteristic	Specific Attributes and Behaviors
		Continually challenges management's analysis and plans.
		Knows when to pick fights and when to give in.
		Is always asking questions.
		Does not hesitate to question management's action after it is taken.
		Does not hesitate to criticize management plans and actions.

Managing Dual Accountability

9.	Recognizes important responsibility to both division *and* corporate management	Understands corporate expectations.
		Recognizes responsibility to corporate management.
		Judgment is recognized by management.
		Is able to judge what is important and what is not.
		Has good rapport with corporate management.
		Is the eyes, ears, and sense of management.

(Exhibit 8-1). Those seeking these other controller roles can therefore use the guidelines by focusing on aspects relevant for their purposes.

The specific attributes and behaviors of strong controllers are detailed in Exhibit 8-3. The list was compiled from words and phrases used by managers in this study when describing their strong controllers. While all the dimensions are important, characteristics 1, 4, 5, 6, 7, and 8 are particularly so for the accomplishment of high controller involvement in business decision making. Characteristics 2 and 3 are vital to the achievement of high controller independence. Characteristic 9 is critical for those seeking high involvement *and* high independence.

How can a company develop controllers with the attributes and behaviors noted in Exhibit 8-3? Based on the experience of those that have done it, the following are some pointers concerning the recruitment, selection, placement, progression, education, training, personnel evaluation, weeding, and career pathing of strong controllers.

Recruitment and Selection

Because both technical and business knowledge are important (characteristics 3, 4, and 5 in Exhibit 8-3), the company can recruit either people with Masters of Business Administration (MBAs) degrees with an accounting background or certified public accountants (CPAs) with a business background for entry-level positions leading to division controllership.[11] In selecting individuals, the company should look not only for a strong accounting and business education background but also for evidence of the personal qualities listed in Exhibit 8-3 (characteristics 1 and 2). The latter are difficult to judge, but progress may be made by having several company managers—both controllers and operating executives—interview the strongest candidates with an eye toward specific activities and indications in the individual's career (for example, extracurricular activities, leadership positions) that provide clues concerning the personal characteristics that are important. Personality tests may be used to *supplement* the collective judgment of the interviewers, but these tests are not reliable enough to be used in isolation. In some cases, their use may lead to legal difficulties if appropriate test validation is lacking. The other characteristics in Exhibit 8-3 cannot be assessed with much confidence when selecting individuals for entry-level positions. They must be evaluated as persons aspiring to division controllership progress within the company.

Placement and Progression

The initial placement should give the individual an opportunity to round out his or her basic technical and business skills; for example, those with strong accounting backgrounds but in need of more business exposure may be placed in the operating divisions, whereas those with the opposite needs may start out in the corporate accounting department. Subsequent moves should attempt to expose the individual more thoroughly to the company's business and operations. Such exposure is important in developing business and communication skills (characteristics 5 and 6 in Exhibit 8-3).

Depending on their particular philosophy and situation, companies may wish to use the corporate internal audit department as a "training ground" for individuals with strong potential. These individuals may be "farmed out" to the operating divisions on a planned basis within two to five years after their initial appointment. There are definite advantages to this approach: an excellent overview of the company's operations for the most promising candidates and an opportunity for them to communicate with managers in a variety of field locations. On the other hand, internal audit may be judged too vital to be used as such a training ground.

[11] A recent survey of 180 division controllers in *Fortune* 500 companies found that 39 (22 percent) had CPAs, 33 percent had MBAs, and 83 percent held a bachelor's degree in business administration (Jannell and Kinnunen, 1980).

Continuing Education and Training

The rapidly changing rules and regulations concerning accounting and auditing requires that the company provide continuing education and training. Both company-sponsored and outside technical programs may be used effectively.

Of equal importance are programs concerned with the development of interpersonal competence and the management of dual accountability (characteristics 7, 8, and 9 in Exhibit 8-3). It could be argued that these skills deserve special emphasis because those attracted to controllership are by nature more "numbers oriented" than "people oriented." Whatever the merits of this argument, it is certainly true that the education and training of would-be controllers does not typically include acquisition of these skills displayed by strong controllers. To provide the interested reader with some guidance, Exhibit 8-4 contains a list of the materials used in short controller training programs. Brief comments on the use of these materials follow to indicate how these or similar materials may be used in the education and training of strong controllers.

In both the Rose Company case and the movie *Twelve O'Clock High,* the central character is given a new work assignment and faces the challenge of building effective working relationships and of developing influence with the new associates.[12] The assigned readings discuss various stages in the development of working relationships (Gabarro) and introduce the notions of dependency, power, and influence (Kotter) that provide useful concepts for those seeking to become strong controllers.

The Thom Sailer case describes the conflict being experienced by a group controller in dealing with a powerful and entrepreneurial division general manager who routinely fails to provide the reports and information requested by the controller. The associated reading describes methods of conflict control and conflict resolution that are helpful in dealing with the conflict situation. The self-administered questionnaire may be used to help individuals assess the extent to which they rely on various modes of conflict resolution—smoothing, forcing, or confrontation. The last mentioned is the dominant conflict resolution mode of strong controllers.

The case on Evaluation of Controllership Effectiveness at ITT describes the company's "solid line" reporting relationship between the corporate and division controllers and outlines the procedure ITT uses to assess controllership effectiveness. This author's *Harvard Business Review* article indicates why the management of dual accountability is of critical importance to controllers, and the paper by Lawrence, Kolodny, and Davis provides helpful concepts for those who must learn to simultaneously manage two bosses. For a more comprehensive discussion of life in a two-boss environment, the reader may consult the book *Matrix* by Davis and

---

[12] I am indebted to Professor Jay W. Lorsch for suggesting these two materials.

Exhibit 8-4   Teaching Materials for a Short Program
on Development of Interpersonal Skills
and Management of Dual Accountability

Topic	Materials	References
Building relationships and developing influence	The Rose Company case "Socialization at the Top" by John J. Gabarro	ICCH[a] 9-453-002 *Organizational Dynamics* (Winter 1979)
	The movie *Twelve O'Clock High*	Films, Inc. 440 Park Avenue South New York, N.Y. 10016
	"Power, Dependence, and Effective Management" by John P. Kotter	*Harvard Business Review* (July-August 1977)
Managing interpersonal conflict	The Thom Sailer case (A) and (B)	ICCH 9-475-098
	"Managing Interpersonal Conflict" by James P. Ware	ICCH 9-479-004
	Self-administered questionnaire on mode of conflict resolution	Variables Q17 and Q18 in the Methodological Appendix
Managing dual accountability	The Evaluation of Controllership Effectiveness at ITT case	ICCH 9-478-002
	"Who Should Control Division Controllers?" by Vijay Sathe	*Harvard Business Review,* (September-October 1978)
	"The Human Side of Matrix" by Lawrence, Kolodny, and Davis	*Organizational Dynamics* (Summer 1977)

[a]Intercollegiate Case Clearing House, Soldiers Field, Boston, Massachusetts 02163.

Lawrence.[13] Chapter 5 of the book, Matrix and the Individual, contains specific skills and development methods to help effectively manage dual accountability.

Personnel Evaluation and Weeding

Companies that are successful in developing large numbers of strong controllers pay careful attention to the evaluation and, for lack of a better term, the weeding of its controllership personnel. The term "weeding" refers to the process of identifying those showing promise of becoming strong controllers. Whereas programs

[13] Davis and Lawrence (1977).

offered in the preceding sections facilitate the development of strong controllers, some of the required characteristics are so demanding that not everyone will be able to acquire the necessary skills. Other characteristics are difficult to assess during selection at the entry level and must be judged on the basis of the individual's subsequent track record. A company must therefore monitor the development of those aspiring to division controllership and pay particular attention to those with the potential for becoming strong controllers.

The approach used by company 14 (see Chapter 2) suggests the kind of effort needed. Their evaluation process yields three categories: "superstars or potential superstars," "very good performers, advancement probable," and "good performers but advancement unlikely." Those selected to become division controllers typically come from the first category. Another company specifically indicates which personnel are available for promotion to division controller by "certifying" those who have demonstrated the required personal qualities and professional and interpersonal skills.

Career Paths

Because active involvement in business decisions and high independence from division management are both required, career paths that offer perspective on why both are important and what the accomplishment of each demands are recommended for individuals with the potential for becoming strong controllers. Thus, movement of personnel within the controllership area between corporate headquarters and the operating divisions as well as personnel transfers from controllership to operating positions should be encouraged. Although the latter may result in the "loss" of some strong candidates to operating positions, this must be accepted if individuals with the qualities and skills required of strong controllers are to be attracted into controllership.

Cross-functional moves in the other direction, that is, moving strong candidates from operating positions into controllership, is more difficult because these candidates typically do not have the necessary accounting background. More important, those in operating positions tend to view transfers into staff jobs such as controllership with disfavor because they are not perceived as offering opportunities for advancement to top management. As one corporate controller put it,

> The pressure that causes staff personnel to seek operating positions is almost always one sided. Seldom do operating managers seek to become staff. Quality attrition of a persistent nature tends to cause a "residual" one-faced personality profile in staff groups. The enthusiastic and energetic leave, and the residual group becomes weighted with individuals of a less dynamic quality. The one-directional flow limits balanced awareness within the corporate totality.

If development of strong controllers is sought, the company must attempt to overcome such stereotypes and the resulting problems by making controllership a viable path to top management. One company sends clear signals that, when senior management appointments are made, those with operating *and* staff experience will be favored over those with experience in only one of the two areas. In another company that has a large proportion of strong controllers, those aspiring to general management positions clearly understand that, to be considered eligible, they must have a demonstrated track record in at least four of the functional areas, that is, marketing, manufacturing, controllership, finance, personnel, purchasing.

Having addressed the questions of what the role of the division controller should be and how strong controllers may be developed, the discussion turns now to the analogous question of what the role of the corporate controller should be.

WHAT SHOULD THE ROLE
OF THE CORPORATE CONTROLLER BE?

Just as the division controller has responsibilities to both division management and to corporate management, so too does the corporate controller to both corporate management and to representatives of the common stockholder, that is, the board of directors. As such, the guidelines in the preceding section designed to aid corporate management in determining the desired role for the company's division controllers can also be used by the board of directors in determining what the role of the corporate controller should be.

The suggested analogy between the roles of the corporate and division controllers may seem inappropriate to managers in companies where the bylaws do not spell out the corporate controller's responsibility to the common stockholders and their legal representatives—the board of directors—or where, through tradition or custom, such responsibility is not considered vital. If this is the case, the purpose here is to provoke a discussion of whether such an arrangement derived from either company law or corporate tradition is really desirable from the standpoint of the common stockholder. It must be emphasized that this discussion is a *logical* extension of the argument in the preceding section. General tendencies and ideals are depicted here that, for a variety of reasons, may not be fully realized in practice. Consider the following account of events at one company.

When asked why the corporate controller personally visited all field locations for quarterly closing of the books—and had done so for the last ten years—the chief executive officer confided, "He is involved in all quarterly closing because there are a lot of areas in which judgment is required. If you want to call it manipulation, fine, but the company needs quarter-to-quarter increases in performance. In a mature business such as ours, the stock price is dependent on the ability to provide *consistent* earnings increases." Whether or not the chief executive officer really understood what the corporate controller was doing with the divisional visit, troublesome ethical and legal questions are raised because someone in corporate management was apparently manipulating ("managing") financial results to show steady growth in an attempt to influence the stock price.

The corporate controller was obviously not discharging his responsibilities in a professional manner, but how could this have been prevented when the chief executive appeared to be responsible for manipulating the results? This question is raised because it is relevant in light of the recent discussion and debate concerning the role of the board of directors in general and that of the audit committee of the board in particular. The latter is responsible for monitoring the integrity of the company's internal controls and the accuracy and fairness of the company's financial reports. But, as one source pointed out in an article in the business press, "Everything is fine as long as there are no problems. But remember, the audit committee is there to prevent a devious management from deceiving the public. So everything is fine until you run into that sort of situation, in which management will try to befuddle the audit committee."[14]

To cope with situations such as this, attempts are being made to give the audit committee some "teeth." For instance, many companies now require outside membership on audit committees. In other companies the corporate internal auditors report jointly to the audit committee of the board and to the corporate management. Some people have proposed that the audit committee be assigned a separate internal audit staff. Others suggest a "private audience" between committee members and the external auditors—an annual or biannual session, in which management does not participate.

All these mechanisms are intended to ensure the independence of the audit committee and to provide it with valid information on company and management performance. These proposals are fine as far as they go, but neither the audit committee nor the external or internal auditors have the depth of knowledge of company operations or the access to sensitive management information and deliberations in progress needed to detect subtle misrepresentations or questionable decisions or actions being contemplated. As one highly regarded corporate controller pointed out, "The audit committee *does not* know and *cannot* know what is really going on! The controller is the knowledgeable guardian—the rest is supportive background and cannot replace his duty to the common shareholder."

If this is a valid analysis, to what extent should the corporate controller's responsibility to the board be emphasized vis-à-vis his or her responsibility to corporate management? By substituting "corporate management" for "division management," "board of directors" for "corporate management," and "corporate controller" for "division controller," Exhibits 8-1 and 8-2 along with the associated discussion in the first section of this chapter provide the board with guidelines for determining what the role of the corporate controller should be. To repeat, this conclusion flows from *logic* and *analogy* and is meant to be provocative. The author recognizes that, for a number of reasons, the suggested ideal may not be fully achieved in actual practice.

[14] "Mr. C.P.A., Meet Mr. C.C.D.," *Forbes*, May 1, 1978, p. 28. The initials C.C.D. stand for certified corporate director, a "degree" given by the National Association of Corporate Directors, a for-profit firm based in Washington, D.C., to directors completing a one-week course aimed at enhancing the proficiency of directors.

As is the case at the division level, the strong controller is potentially the most effective role at the corporate level. It opens up the possibility of "before-the-fact" or anticipatory control, something that no other type of controller role offers. Just as the division controller who remains involved while retaining independence is a more effective local guardian than one who is independent but not involved, so too is the corporate controller who can overcome the apparent tension between involvement and independence. The role is difficult to perform. It requires the selection and retention of a "strong" corporate controller—one with personal integrity, high professional standards, maturity, good business judgment, and communication skills. Business judgment and communication skills are needed to speak the language of management and to contribute actively in business decisions. With such active participation comes access to all sensitive discussions and deliberations in progress as well as an in-depth understanding of management's attitude and thinking. Personal integrity, professionalism, and maturity are needed to know when management has overstepped the bounds of reasonable conduct and to take the necessary action, that is, to inform the board of directors.

While acknowledging the need for more responsive, before-the-fact control, many would argue that the way to accomplish this is by holding *corporate management* accountable, not by relying on the corporate controller. Corporate management is, of course, accountable to the board of directors for decisions affecting these and other areas of responsibility. But the board is also accountable to the stockholders and the general public for corporate performance, and the liability exposure that such accountability entails has been on the rise. Until recently, personal liability was limited to actions known to the board. Liability seems to be extending to matters that the board *should* have known about. This broader interpretation increases the importance of securing valid information from management before it is too late. Board members may therefore seek a system of checks and balances in areas of particular concern to them.

But who is to check on the board itself? What if the board suspects the management is misrepresenting the company to its stockholders and the general public but does nothing about it? This is not a remote possibility, particularly if the chief executive officer is domineering. It follows *logically* from the earlier discussion and leads us to the heart of the question of corporate accountability. The basic issue raised is this: Where does one ultimately peg corporate accountability?

On analysis and reflection, one is forced to conclude that the checking on the checkers has to end somewhere. The board represents the logical and practical dead end in the quest for ultimate accountability. The stockholders are neither knowledgeable nor organized to personally monitor the activities of the corporation or the board (even if they wished to do so). Their best bet is to ensure that only strong individuals—those with some knowledge of business, strength of personal character, and an indepedence of mind—serve on the board.

The concluding section of the book considers the study implications for other staff roles in management.

WHAT SHOULD THE STAFF ROLE IN MANAGEMENT BE?

Some would argue that the question is redundant because the line-staff distinction is obsolete. Those taking this position have in mind the traditional definition of line roles as those responsible for the "primary" objectives of the enterprise and staff roles being those supporting the primary ones. By this definition, production and sales (and sometimes engineering and finance) are classified as line positions, whereas positions in accounting, control, legal, personnel, purchasing, public relations, quality assurance, and research are classified as staff.

The problem with such a definition is that it leads to futile debates over which roles are to be considered primary to the objectives of the enterprise. For instance, is the purchasing of crude oil any less of a primary function for the oil companies than is its processing and sale? And as the experience with the DC-10 jumbo jet indicates, no role could be judged more essential than quality control for manufacturers of commercial aircraft. Those who view the traditional line-staff distinction as obsolete argue that the successful management of the modern enterprise requires the effective collaboration of a variety of disciplines. Distinctions attempting to segregate these into ones of primary and secondary importance serve no useful purpose. Because this position is endorsed by the author, the definition of staff roles given now should be noted.

The typical contemporary corporation is composed of several business units ("divisions") serving particular market segments with certain products and/or services. The head of each division, the division general manager, reports to the chief executive officer of the corporation, frequently through one or more intermediate general management levels, and is responsible for the overall performance of the division. Reporting to the general managers at each level are one or more functions such as engineering, control, finance, marketing, personnel, production, sales, and quality control. Some of these functions are responsible for operational work, that is, for the development, production, and sale of the business unit's products and/or services. The managers of these functions, the operating executives, perform what are called operating roles in this book, for example, manufacturing, sales. Other functions are responsible for specialist work, that is, for assisting and monitoring the performance of operational work, for example, controller, personnel, legal.

Thus, this definition of staff roles does not hinge on whether the function is to be considered of primary or secondary importance. Both operating and staff roles are important—or they would not exist—and distinctions based on degree of importance serve no useful purpose. Neither is this definition of staff roles based on differences in formal authority. Both operating and staff roles have authority in their areas of activity. Rather, the distinction made is based on the kind of behavior demanded of those performing these roles. Operating roles are concerned with the development, production, and sale of the business unit's products and for services.

Staff roles are concerned with assisting and/or monitoring the performance of these activities.

So defined, staff roles can hardly be considered obsolete. A company of any size has several of them; in a large corporation there are literally hundreds of such positions. And they exist for a very good reason. The general managers and operating executives, however bright and capable, simply do not have the depth of knowledge in the variety of disciplines needed for effective management in the contemporary business environment. The difficulty stems not just from size and the associated requirement for division of labor. The management task is *complex* enough that these individuals typically do not have the variety of skills and expertise needed to perform it with maximum effectiveness. Given the need for staff as defined here, what should the staff role in management be?

One important aspect of staff roles was just mentioned. Because of increasing organizational size and complexity, the importance of the staff contribution in business decisions has increased enormously. A staff actively involved increases the likelihood that appropriate specialist knowledge, expertise, and judgment will be brought to bear when these decisions are made. The rationale was developed more fully in Chapter 1 (see Literature on Line and Staff) and is not repeated here.

Another important aspect of some staff roles is the responsibility for ensuring compliance with corporate policies, procedures, and standards. The controller, for instance, is responsible for ensuring that local control practices conform to corporate policy and procedures, which in turn are dictated in part by auditing rules and financial reporting requirements specified by governmental agencies and regulatory bodies (for example, IRS, SEC). As the corporation experiences mounting external pressures from litigation and regulation, the monitoring aspect of other staff roles is also gaining importance. For instance, because of increased exposure to product liability claims, it is becoming increasingly important that quality control staff and legal staff take steps to ensure compliance with appropriate standards. Similarly, personnel staff must ensure compliance with increased government regulation concerning equal employment opportunity, occupational safety and health, and other areas of concern.

Although general managers at each level are fully accountable to general management at higher levels for these and other areas of responsibility, higher-level management may seek a system of checks and balances in areas of particular concern to them. If this were not so, there would be no need for an internal audit function, for instance. Many corporations chose to install such a function because of particular concern with the maintenance of internal control. As other concerns gain similar importance, management may desire a method of checks and balances in these areas as well.

The underlying motivation may not be fully appreciated by those unfamiliar with the contemporary legal environment in which business operates. Personal liability today is generally perceived to be an expanding concept—management is not only liable for *known* actions and decisions but increasingly for those it *should have* known about and had the power to prevent. This expanding interpretation of liability without culpability increases the importance for each level of management of securing valid information from lower management levels concerning decisions and actions for which they are potentially liable—preferably *before* they are taken. Hence, the understandable need for a system of checks and balances.

As the preceding discussion indicates, staff roles in management have two important facets: contributing to business decisions requiring active involvement in management and monitoring compliance with corporate policies, procedures, and standards requiring a degree of objectivity and independence in dealing with affiliated management. Since the degree of importance of one of these facets versus the other may vary from one staff role to another at the same general management level, from one general management level to another within the same company, and from company to company, managers must determine what the staff roles should be in light of their own particular circumstances.

Exhibit 8-5   Criteria That Management at Any Level Can Use to Determine What a Staff Role at the Next Lower Management Level Should Be

---

Required Emphasis on the Staff Role's Management Service Responsibility
at the Next Lower Management Level
(higher scores argue for greater emphasis)

---

1. Net benefits from the staff role's potential contribution in business decisions at the next lower management level in relation to the potential costs of stifled management creativity and initiative

1	2	3	4	5
Limited		Moderate		Considerable

2. Next lower level general management's expertise in the area of the staff role's potential contribution

5	4	3	2	1
Limited		Moderate		Considerable

Required Emphasis on Staff Role's Responsibility for Monitoring Compliance
with Corporate Policies, Procedures, and Standards
(higher scores argue for greater emphasis)

---

1. Importance of compliance with policies, procedures, and standards in the staff role's areas of responsibility

1	2	3	4	5
Limited		Moderate		Considerable

2. Confidence in the integrity and good judgment of management at the next lower level

5	4	3	2	1
Limited		Moderate		Considerable

The criteria summarized in Exhibit 8-5 (generalized from Exhibit 8-2) provide managers at any organizational level with a method for systematically assessing what the staff roles at the next lower management level should be. Since the procedure exactly parallels that described for Exhibit 8-2, it is not repeated. It gives management an indication of the relative emphasis that should be placed on the two facets of staff roles at the next lower level of management. Such an assessment then leads to the choice of role type in Exhibit 8-1 best suited to one's own situation. It should be noted that these recommendations, like the ones made for the role of the corporate controller, derive from *analogy* and are a *logical* extension of the arguments made for the role of the division controller. They are meant to provoke a thoughtful discussion of the topic, and should be regarded as suggestive rather than definitive.

As has been discussed, the strong staff role calling for high emphasis on both the management service and the monitoring compliance responsibilities is the only one that offers the promise of "before-the-fact," or anticipatory, control. One cost, however, is the time and resources needed to develop "strong" staff, those able to remain actively involved in business decisions while retaining a sense of objectivity and independence in dealing with affiliated management. Another cost is the potential danger of stifling the creativity and initiative of operating management. The extent to which this actually materializes depends on the prevailing managerial approach and interpersonal relationships, as discussed previously. Companies interested in the development of strong staff should engage in a program of selection, placement, education, training, and career planning analogous to the one described earlier for the development of strong controllers.

Methodological Appendix

VARIABLE INDEX

Nomenclature

Prefix "D" indicates that variable is measured via documents.
Prefix "Q" indicates that variable is measured via questionnaire.
Prefix "I" indicates that variable is measured via interview question.

Variable Number	Variable Name	Page Number
D1	Company financial performance relative to the industry	158
D2	Company financial stress	158
D3	Company operating interdependence	158
D4	Chief executive officer has financial background	158
D5	Percentage of senior corporate executives with financial backgrounds	158
D6	Capital asset intensity	159
D7	Working asset intensity	159
D8	Operating margin (*reversed scale*)	159
Q1	Division management's expectations regarding division controller involvement	160

155

Variable Number	Variable Name	Page Number
Q2	Corporate management's expectations regarding corporate controller involvement	160
Q3	Corporate management's expectations regarding *typical* division controller management	160
Q4	Corporate controller's expectations regarding *typical* division controller involvement	160
Q5	Degree of division controller involvement in business decisions	160
Q6	Degree of corporate controller involvement in business decisions	160
Q7	Degree of *typical* division controller involvement in business decisions	160
Q8	Scope of division controller involvement in business decisions	161
Q9	Overall rate of change of corporate business environment	161
Q10	Number of aspects of the corporate business environment subject to rapid change	161
Q11	Composite index of rate of corporate environmental change	161
Q12	Overall rate of change of divisional business environment	161
Q13	Number of aspects of divisional business environment subject to rapid change	161
Q14	Composite index of rate of change of divisional business environment	161
Q15	Management's emphasis on planning, budgeting, and capital expenditure reviews	164
Q16	Degree of the corporate controller's formal authority over the division controllers	165
Q17	Corporate controller's reliance on the confrontation mode in conflict resolution	167
Q18	Division controller's reliance on the confrontation mode in conflict resolution	167
Q19	Proportion of time spent by the corporate controller on the external reporting responsibilities	168
Q20	Proportion of time spent by the division controller on the external reporting responsibilities	168
Q21	Proportion of time spent by the corporate	

Variable Number	Variable Name	Page Number
	controller's headquarters staff on division management reports and requests	168
Q22	Corporate management's expectations regarding controller independence	169
Q23	Division management's expectations regarding controller independence	169
I1	Management's concern about the integrity of financial reporting and/or the adequacy of internal control	170
I2	Strength of internal audit	170
I3	Audit as training ground	170
I4	Personnel executives assigned to controllership	171
I5	Corporate controller's own involvement in the development of controllership personnel	171
I6	Duration of sustained emphasis on development of controllership personnel	171
I7	Controllership to line transfers	172
I8	Corporate management's financial orientation	172

INTRODUCTION TO THE APPENDIX

The material that follows is intended to give the reader necessary details concerning the specific questions asked in the interviews and in the questionnaires, along with a description of how the responses are used to obtain the various measurements. Interview checklists that yielded the qualitative materials for this study are also included. Unless a source is cited, the questions have been developed by the author for this study.

The following abbreviations are used throughout:

CEO - Chief executive officer
CM - Corporate managers reporting to the CEO
CC - Corporate controller
DGM - Division general manager
DM - Division managers reporting to the DGM
DC - Division controller

The appendix is organized as follows. Variables measured from company documents and publications are presented first, followed by variables scaled via the questionnaires. Variables measured via interview questions are included next. Finally, checklists of items covered in the various interviews are presented.

VARIABLES MEASURED
VIA PUBLISHED DOCUMENTS

The variables whose measurement is based on company annual reports and other documents are as follows. Variable numbers are prefixed by the letter "D" to indicate that the measurement is based on documents.

Variable D1: Company Financial Performance
Relative to the Industry

This measurement is based on four factors: (1) average return on sales during the last five years, (2) average return on equity during the last five years, (3) percentage change in net profit after taxes over the last five years, and (4) percentage change in sales over the last five years. Company scores for these four factors are compared with the corresponding scores for the company's industry competitors. If a factor score for the company is below the corresponding industry average, it is assigned a value of 1, if at or above the industry average a value of 2. Combining the values for the four factors yields a minimum value of 4 (all factors valued at 1) and a maximum value of 8 (all factors valued at 2) and results in the following scale of company financial performance relative to the industry: 1 = performance considerably below average (total of factor values = 4), 2 = below average (5), 3 = average (6), 4 = above average (7), and 5 = considerably above average (8). (Source: Company and industry financial reports.)

Variable D2: Company Financial Stress

A company is considered to be experiencing financial stress if the decline in profits or sales from one year to the next is greater than 20 percent during more than one of the previous five years and/or the retained earnings is a negative figure during one of the previous five years. Profit for the purposes of these calculations is net profit after taxes and before extraordinary items. Thus, the scale used is nonstress situation = 1, stress situation = 2. (Source: Company annual reports.)

Variable D3: Company Operating Interdependence

Company operating interdependence is measured by the volume of intracompany sales as a percentage of total company sales during the most recent financial year. (Source: Company documents.)

Variables D4 and D5:
Management's Financial Background

A manager is considered to have a financial background if he or she has had formal education in accounting and/or at least ten years of experience in the accounting and controllership area. (Source: Company documents and *Dun and*

158

Bradstreet reports.) Based on this definition, variables D4 and D5 are measured as follows:

Variable Number	Variable Name	Variable Measurement
D4	CEO has a financial background	No = 1 Yes = 2
D5	Percentage of senior corporate executives with financial backgrounds	Percentage of the corporate officers that have a financial background

Variables D6-D8: Criticality of Financial Analyses and Control

The following financial ratios for the most recent financial year are used as surrogates for the degree to which financial analysis and control are critical to business success. (Source: Company annual reports.)

Variable Number	Variable Name	Computation Procedure
D6	Capital asset intensity	Fixed assets divided by net sales
D7	Working asset intensity	Inventories plus receivables divided by net sales
D8	Operating margin (*reversed scale:* low margin = high criticality of financial analysis and control)	Operating income (that is, net sales less operating expenses) divided by net sales

VARIABLES MEASURED VIA QUESTIONNAIRES

In some of the questionnaires for this study, the same basic question was asked of more than one individual or was used to measure more than one variable. In these cases the exact wording of the questions was altered to fit the organizational level (corporate versus division) and position (controller versus other manager) of the respondent. For reasons of economy and convenience, however, all these variations are not reproduced here. Instead, one example of the basic question is given, followed by a description of the variables, the executives completing each, and the procedure used to compute variable scores.

The following practice is adopted in scoring variables from the questionnaire responses. For a variable measured by responses from a single individual, the absence of any one response (indicated by a blank, or by the response "NB," no basis for opinion) leads to the variable's being not scored for the division or company in question. For a variable measured by averaging more than one individual's responses, a nonresponse leads to that particular individual's exclusion from the averaging process. Variable numbers are prefixed by the letter "Q" to indicate that these measures are derived from questionnaires.

Variables Q1-Q7: Degree of Controller Involvement, Expected and Actual

Different division managers have different expectations concerning the role that their division controllers should perform. Please use the scale following to indicate your expectations regarding your division controller's role and your opinion of how the role is actually performed.

Rating Scale

1. Very undescriptive
2. Somewhat undescriptive
3. Somewhat descriptive
4. Very descriptive
NB. No basis for opinion

	Expected Role	Actual Role
Role of participant in *operating* business decisions (impact within one year)		
Present information and analysis	_____	_____
Recommend action that should be taken	_____	_____
Challenge plans and actions of operating executives	_____	_____
Role of participant in *strategic* business decisions (impact over two or more years)		
Present information and analysis	_____	_____
Recommend action that should be taken	_____	_____
Challenge plans and actions of operating executives	_____	_____

The procedure used for measuring the different variables is indicated as follows:

Variable Number	Variable Name	Respondents	Computation Procedure
Q1	Division management's expectations regarding division controller involvement	DGM	Add ratings in the expected role column
Q2	Corporate management's expectations regarding corporate controller involvement	CEO	Same as above
Q3	Corporate management's expectations regarding *typical* division controller involvement	CEO	Same as above
Q4	Corporate controller's expectations regarding *typical* division controller involvement	CC	Same as above
Q5	Degree of division controller involvement in business decisions	DGM and DMs	Add ratings in the actual role column for each respondent and compute average
Q6	Degree of corporate controller involvement in business decisions	CEO and CMs	Same as above
Q7	Degree of *typical* division controller involvement in business decisions	CEO and CMs	Same as above

Note: The "low," "moderate," and "high" degrees of controller involvement referred to in Exhibits 2-1 through 2-5 result from trichotomizing scores for variables Q6 and Q7.

Variable Q8: Scope of Division Controller Involvement

For a number of reasons (for example, nature of the business, company tradition) the role actually performed by the division controller varies from one division to another. We are interested in understanding the situation as it exists in *your division*.

What role does the division controller actually perform when *key* decisions are made in each of the areas listed? (See page 162.)

Variables Q9-Q14: Rate of Change of Business Environment

Corporations differ in terms of the rate at which the business environments in which they operate change. Although there may be differences from one division

161

Role of Division Controller

Decision Areas	Has no Role in the Decision-Making Process 1	His Opinion is Solicited Prior to Decisions Being Made by Others 2	Is a *Minor* Participant in Decision Making 3	Is a *Major* Participant in Decision Making 4	Is the Sole Decision Maker 5	No Basis for Opinion NB	Decision Is Not Made in the Division NM
Advertising	1	2	3	4	5	NB	NM
Promotion	1	2	3	4	5	NB	NM
Distribution	1	2	3	4	5	NB	NM
Acquisition and mergers	1	2	3	4	5	NB	NM
New product development	1	2	3	4	5	NB	NM
Capital investment	1	2	3	4	5	NB	NM
Selection of executives outside the controllership area	1	2	3	4	5	NB	NM
Credit policy	1	2	3	4	5	NB	NM
Pricing policy	1	2	3	4	5	NB	NM
Inventory policy	1	2	3	4	5	NB	NM
Settling customer claims	1	2	3	4	5	NB	NM
Stopping customer deliveries	1	2	3	4	5	NB	NM

Variable Name	*Respondent*	*Computation Procedure*
Scope of division controller involvement in business decisions	DGM	Count the number of decision areas circled 3, 4, or 5

Variable Number

Q8

to another within the same corporation also, we are interested only in getting a rough idea of the overall differences that exist between various corporations in this regard. *Using the past five years as a point of reference,* please give us your opinion of the rate at which important changes have occurred in various aspects of the business environment of your *corporation as a whole.*

	Rate of Change					*No Basis for Opinion*
	Slow		Moderate		Rapid	
Aspect of Business Environment						
1. Customer buying patterns and requirements	1	2	3	4	5	NB
2. Distributor attitudes and requirements	1	2	3	4	5	NB
3. Government regulations and reporting requirements	1	2	3	4	5	NB
4. Technical developments relevant to the corporation's businesses	1	2	3	4	5	NB
5. Supply sources						
Capital markets	1	2	3	4	5	NB
Raw material markets	1	2	3	4	5	NB
Labor markets	1	2	3	4	5	NB
6. Competitors actions						
Product innovation	1	2	3	4	5	NB
Advertising	1	2	3	4	5	NB
Distribution	1	2	3	4	5	NB
Pricing	1	2	3	4	5	NB
7. Overall	1	2	3	4	5	NB

J. W. Lorsch and Stephen A. Allen, III, *Managing Diversity and Interdependence: An Organizational Study of Multi-Divisional Firms* (Boston: Division of Research, Harvard Business School, 1973), p. 235.

The procedure used to measure the different variables is indicated as follows:

Variable Number	Variable Name	Respondent	Computation Procedure
Q9	Overall rate of change of corporate business environment	CEO	Record rating given on line 7
Q10	Number of aspects of the corporate business environment subject to rapid change	CEO	Count the number of aspects rated 4 or 5

Variable Number	Variable Name	Respondent	Computation Procedure
Q11	Composite index of rate of corporate environmental change	CEO	Variable Q9 multiplied by variable Q10
Q12	Overall rate of change of divisional business environment	DGM	Record rating given on line 7
Q13	Number of aspects of divisional business environment subject to rapid change	DGM	Count the number of aspects rated 4 or 5
Q14	Composite index of rate of divisional environmental change	DGM	Variable Q12 multiplied by variable Q13

Variable Q15: Management's Emphasis on Planning, Budgeting, and Capital Expenditure Review

Listed are several "organizational devices" that are frequently used for managing relationships between the corporate headquarters and the divisions. We'd like to know the relative importance corporate top management places on these devices in managing corporate-division relationships in your company.

	Not Used	Importance					No Basis for Opinion
		Limited		Moderate		Extreme	
Organizational Device	NU	1	2	3	4	5	NB
1. Annual budgeting system	NU	1	2	3	4	5	NB
2. Long-range planning system	NU	1	2	3	4	5	NB
3. Approval system for major capital and expense items	NU	1	2	3	4	5	NB
4. Monthly budget review	NU	1	2	3	4	5	NB
5. Monthly narrative reports on operations	NU	1	2	3	4	5	NB
6. Formal goal-setting system	NU	1	2	3	4	5	NB
7. Performance evaluation and incentive compensation system for divisional executives	NU	1	2	3	4	5	NB

	Not Used	Importance					No Basis for Opinion
		Limited		Moderate		Extreme	
8. Direct informal contacts between corporate and divisional executives	NU	1	2	3	4	5	NB
9. Interdivisional task forces and committees	NU	1	2	3	4	5	NB
10. Corporate and divisional task forces and committees	NU	1	2	3	4	5	NB
11. Group or operating vice presidents	NU	1	2	3	4	5	NB
12. Other full-time employees responsible for interdivisional coordination	NU	1	2	3	4	5	NB
13. Planned interdivisional and corporate and divisional transfers of executive personnel	NU	1	2	3	4	5	NB

Stephen A. Allen, "Organizational Choices and General Management Influence Networks in Divisionalized Companies," *Academy of Management Journal,* 21, no. 3 (September 1978), 348. Variable Q15 is Allen's factor I—planning, budgeting, and information exchange mechanisms.

Variable Number	Variable Name	Respondents	Computation Procedure
Q15	Management's emphasis on planning, budgeting, and capital expenditures review	CMs	Add responses for lines 1, 2, 3, 7, and 8 above for each respondent and compute average for all CMs combined

Variable Q16: Degree of the Corporate Conroller's Formal Authority over the Division Controller

Although decisions regarding the divisional controller are frequently made after consultation between the corporate controller and the divisional general manager, one of them retains control in the areas indicated. Please indicate who has the *greater authority* when decisions are actually made by checking *one* box for each item:

	Executive Who Has the Greater Authority		
	Divisional General Manager	Corporate Controller	Both Executives Have *Exactly* Equal Authority
1. Hiring of the division controller	☐	☐	☐
2. Transfer of the division controller	☐	☐	☐
3. Promotion of the division controller	☐	☐	☐
4. Salary increase for the division controller	☐	☐	☐
5. Bonus for the division controller (if applicable)	☐	☐	☐
6. Termination of the division controller	☐	☐	☐
7. Physical location of the division controller	☐	☐	☐
8. Determining priorities for work to be done by the division controller	☐	☐	☐
9. Determining the time to be spent by the division controller on various projects	☐	☐	☐

Variable Number	Variable Name	Respondents	Computation Procedure
Q16	Degree of the corporate controller's formal authority over the division controllers	CC and DGMs	Use following scale: DGM has greater authority = 1, both have equal authority = 2, CC has greater authority = 3. Add lines 1 through 9 for each respondent and compute average for all respondents combined

Variables Q17 and Q18: Reliance on
Confrontation Mode in Conflict Resolution

The proverbs listed can be thought of as descriptions of some of the different possibilities for resolving disagreements, as they have been stated in the literature and in traditional wisdom. As you read these proverbs, please indicate, using the following scale, the extent to which they describe *your actual behavior when disagreements arise in dealing with work associates.*

How Frequently Do Each of the Proverbs Listed Describe Your Actual Behavior	Rating Scale				
	Almost Never	Rarely	Sometimes	Often	Almost Always
1. Soft words win hard hearts	1	2	3	4	5
2. Come now and let us reason together	1	2	3	4	5
3. A question must be decided by knowledge and not by numbers if it is to have a right decision	1	2	3	4	5
4. When one hits you with a stone, hit him with a piece of cotton	1	2	3	4	5
5. The arguments of the strongest have always the most weight	1	2	3	4	5
6. By digging and digging, the truth is discovered	1	2	3	4	5
7. Smooth words make smooth ways	1	2	3	4	5
8. If you cannot make a man think as you do, make him do as you think	1	2	3	4	5
9. He who fights and runs away lives to run another day	1	2	3	4	5
10. Might overcomes right	1	2	3	4	5
11. Seek till you find, and you'll not lose your labor	1	2	3	4	5
12. Kill your enemies with kindness	1	2	3	4	5

Paul R. Lawrence and Jay W. Lorsch, *Organization and Environment: Managing Differentiation and Integration* (Boston: Division of Research, Harvard Business School, 1967), p. 265.

The following coding procedure is used to determine reliance on various modes in conflict resolution:

Forcing	Items 5, 8, 9, 10
Smoothing	Items 1, 4, 7, 12
Confrontation	Items 2, 3, 6, 11

Variables Q17 and Q18 are measured as follows:

Variable Number	Variable Name	Respondent	Computation Procedure
Q17	Corporate controller's reliance on the confrontation mode in conflict resolution	CC	Add responses to items 2, 3, 6, and 11
Q18	Division controller's reliance on the confrontation mode in conflict resolution	DC	Same as above

Variables Q19-Q21: Proportion of Time Spent on Various Activities by Controllers and their Staffs

We would like to get a rough idea of how much time is spent by the corporate controller and his or her staff on various requests. Please give us an approximate breakdown of how the total "labor-hours" available last year were spent.

Time Spent (broken down by source of request)	Approximate % Breakdown of Total "Labor-Hours" Available Last Year	
	Corporate Controller	Corporate Controller's Headquarters Staff
1. On requests and reports for external agencies (for example, IRS, SEC)	_____ %	_____ %
2. On requests and reports for corporate top management	_____ %	_____ %
3. On requests and reports for division management	_____ %	_____ %
4. Other (if any)		
_____	_____ %	_____ %
Total	100%	100%

The variables were measured as follows:

Variable Number	Variable Name	Respondents	Computation Procedure
Q19	Proportion of time spent by the corporate controller on the external reporting responsibilities	CC	Line 1 under the corporate controller column
Q20	Proportion of time spent by the division controller on the external reporting responsibilities	DC	Line 1 under the division controller column
Q21	Proportion of time spent by the corporate controller's headquarters staff on divisional management's reports and requests.	CC	Line 2 under the corporate controller's headquarters staff column

Variables Q22 and Q23: Management's Expectations Regarding Controller Independence

Please use the following scale to indicate the extent to which the statement that follows is descriptive of *your* expectations concerning your controller's role:

The controller's role is that of an "umpire in a ballgame"—the reporter of events, calling the results as they come out in as unbiased and fair a manner as possible (circle one number)	Very Undescriptive	Somewhat Undescriptive	Somewhat Descriptive	Very Descriptive
	1	2	3	4

The following variables are computed using the preceding:

Variable Number	Variable Name	Respondents	Computation Procedure
Q22	Corporate management's expectations regarding controller independence	CEO and CMs	Compute an average of all the respondents' scores
Q23	Division management's expectations regarding controller independence	DGM and DMs	Same as above

VARIABLES MEASURED
VIA INTERVIEW QUESTIONS

The variables included in this section are scaled from responses obtained during the interviews. There are two reasons why these questions are not included in the questionnaires. First, the importance of some of these variables emerged as the study progressed and an effort to more systematically measure them was made only during the later field work. Second, if the subject matter was of a sensitive nature, for example, defalcation or financial mismanagement, the question was reserved for the interviews. These variables are numbered with the prefix "I" to indicate the measurement is based on interview questions.

Variable I1: Management Concern About
the Integrity of Financial Reporting
and/or the Adequacy of Internal Control

> As far as you know, has the company experienced either of the following "surprises" during the past five years: (1) the discovery of fraud, defalcation, or illegal payments by company personnel (2) "accounting surprises" or "blowups," for example, *unexpected* write-offs of inventory or receivables having a *significant* adverse impact on corporate profit?

The question was asked of the following executives: CEO, CC, DGMs, DCs, head of internal audit, and the executive working most closely with the company's financial control system. Management concern about the integrity of financial reporting and/or internal control was considered to be acute (score = 2) if there was some consensus that the company had experienced one or more major surprises during the past five years. In all other cases the concern was deemed to be normal (score = 1).

Variable I2: Strength of Internal Audit

> How would you rate the company's internal audit function on a scale of poor = 1, satisfactory = 3, and excellent = 5?

The question was asked of the following executives: CEO, CMs, and DGMs. Variable I2 was measured by computing the average of all these responses.

Variable I3: Audit as Training Ground

> Is the audit function regularly used as a training ground for people seeking other careers within the company, or do you hire and staff the function primarily with career auditors?

170

The question was asked of the CC, DCs, and the head of internal audit. Based on the consensus of these responses, variable I3 was scored as follows: audit not used as training ground = 1, audit used as training ground = 2.

Variable I4: Personnel Executive Assigned to Controllership

Are there one or more executives—either within the controllership area or within the personnel area—who spend *all their time* on matters relating to the selection, training, and development of controllership personnel within the company?

The question was asked of the CC, the DCs, and the personnel executive most familiar with the company's controllers. Based on the information obtained, variable I4 was scaled as follows: no full-time personnel executive devoted to controllership matters = 1, one or more such executives = 2.

Variable I5: Corporate Controller's Own Involvement in the Development of Controllership Personnel

To what extent is the corporate controller personally involved in matters such as placement, career planning, job rotation, and management development of controllership personnel?

The question was asked of the CC, the DCs, and the personnel executive most familiar with the company's controllers. Based on these responses, variable I5 was scored as follows: not highly involved = 1, highly involved = 2.

Variable I6: Duration of Sustained Emphasis on Development of Controllership Personnel

How long has the company had career planning, job rotation, or other programs concerned specifically with the development of personnel in the controllership function?

The question was asked of the CC, the DCs, and the personnel executive most familiar with the company's controllers. Based on the consensus of their responses, variable I6 was given one of the following scores: Such programs are not in place = 1, in place less than two years = 2, in place two to five years = 3, in place five to ten years = 4, in place more than ten years = 5.

Variable I7: Controllership to Line Transfers

> How many division controllers in this company have been transferred to positions in operations, marketing, or general management within the company during the last five years? What are their names?

The question was asked of the CC and the personnel executive most familiar with the company's controllers. Variable 17 is scored as follows: no division controllers were so transferred = 1, one to five were transferred = 2, more than five were transferred = 3.

Variable I8: Corporate Management's Financial Orientation

> To what extent does the corporate management rely on financial information, analysis, and control in their management approach?

The question was asked of the CC, the executive working most closely with the company's financial control system, and the DCs. Based on these responses, the following scores were assigned to variable I8: Corporate management's financial orientation was considered to be high (score = 2), if there was some consensus in the interview responses that management relied heavily on financial information, analysis, and control. In all other cases management's financial orientation was considered to be not high (score = 1).

CHECKLISTS OF INTERVIEW QUESTIONS

Included in this last section of the Methodological Appendix are checklists used during the interview process. Separate checklists were made for persons in each major position interviewed, for example, CC, DC, CEO, DGM. To eliminate redundancy, however, the following procedure is used. The items that were covered with all interviewees are included first. Those that were used for specific positions only are included next. Questions elaborating on prior sections of the appendix dealing with measurement of variables are *not* repeated here.

Items Covered with All Interviewees

1. I would like to begin by briefly describing the broad purpose of this study and how the data collected will be used. You can be assured that our conversation, as well as your responses on the questionnaire, will be treated as strictly confidential. Neither company nor individual names will be identified when the study results are published.
2. Could you tell me a little bit about your background—how long with the company, present job, and so on—and your current major responsibilities?

3. Before going into more specific questions, could we talk about the questionnaire sent to you earlier? I would like to take a look at your responses and to ask you to give me some examples and elaborate where necessary to be sure I correctly understand your views.

4. How would you rate the controllership function here (poor = 1 to outstanding = 10)? What is effective controllership (results, examples)? Good people are important, of course, but what other factors account for different degrees of controllership effectiveness?

5. Technical ability is naturally important, but, at the level of skills, tactics, modes of operation, what does an effective controller do that a less effective one does not? Could you describe some difficult situations and how an effective controller has or would deal with them?

6. Can a company do anything to develop effective controllers? What is being done in your company? What are the typical career paths of controllers in your company?

7. How important is the question of reporting relationships, that is, "solid line" versus "dotted line," between the corporate and division controllers for controller effectiveness? Does the choice really matter in terms of how the controller performs his or her role? Why do companies sometimes change the reporting relationship? Could you articulate the pros and cons? What are the associated career implications for controllers?

8. How would you generally characterize the interpersonal relationships between controllers and other managers in this company for the following: trust, openness, credibility, confidence, allowing errors, accepting blame?

9. What significant changes, if any, have taken place during the past five years with regard to controllers in your company? Specifically, has the controller's influence in management changed? How? Why?

10. What major issues and problems does your company (division) currently face? What is the role of the company's division controllers? As you look ahead to the next five years, what basic issues do you see facing the company (division)? How would these affect controllership? Overall control in the company?

Additional Checklist for CEO, CMs, DGM, and DMs Only

1. Could you help me to understand the nature of the major businesses you are in—the key success factors, key decisions? What is the role of the controller in these?

2. Does your business situation or strategy make the role of controllers here particularly difficult or unique in any way? Capital crunch? Pressures from financial community? Inflation? Profit slide or other crises?

3. What is the relative importance of research and development, marketing, and cost control in your businesses? How does this affect the controller's role?

4. How unpredictable is your business environment in the short run (one year)? In the longer run (five years)?

5. What is the level of interdependence among your divisions in terms of products being transferred from one division to another, competition in the same market(s), identical sources of supply for major items, and so on? How do you achieve coordination between divisions? What is the controller's role in this?

6. Could you briefly describe the nature and extent of your relationships with each of the following groups: financial and accounting people at corporate headquarters, financial and accounting people at divisional level, operating people at corporate headquarters, operating people at divisional level.

Additional Checklist for the CC, the DCs, and Other Controllership Personnel Only

1. Could we talk a little bit about the people reporting to you?
    How many? How organized?
    Qualifications: percentage accounting, percentage BS/BBA, percentage MBA?
    Current recruitment, training: where hired, how trained?
    Career paths: rotation via operations? vice versa?
    Evaluation and rewards: specific details about money, promotions, hire/ fire decisions?
    Stable level of employment or changing?
2. As you see it regarding *your job,* what are
    The keys to success, that is, effectiveness? What factors influence these?
    Some major issues and concerns currently (your headaches)? How do you deal with them?
    Future issues you see as crucial? Your probable response?
3. What factors facilitate or hinder effective use of financial data and analyses by operating executives? How would you characterize the management style of your company's (division's) CEO (DGM)?
4. Could you describe how the audit function is carried out in your company (division)? What is its relationship to the controllership function?

Additional Checklist for the CC Only

1. Could you briefly describe what key events, negotiations, and decisions led to each of the following when they last occurred, and how they affected controllership performance?
    Hiring of division controller.
    Transfer of division controller.
    Promotion of division controller.
    Termination of division controller.
    Salary increase for division controller.
    Award of bonus for division controller.
    Changing the physical location of the division controller.
    Determining time and work priorities (corporate versus division requests) of the division controller.
    Submitting divisional performance reports to corporate headquarters.
    Submitting divisional budgets for corporate approval.
    Filing of reports by the division controller with corporate headquarters without informing divisional management (periodic variance reports, other).

Modification of the standard companywide accounting and control system to better serve the needs of the division.

Obtaining additional staffing authorization.

Resolution of a serious difference of opinion or conflict between (a) divisional controller and corporate controller, (b) divisional controller and divisional general manager.

Detection of fraud or financial mismanagement in one of the divisions.

Major change in the financial control system.

2. What are some typical problems that your division controllers face? How do they cope with these problems? What is it that makes some of your controllers more effective than others?

Additional Checklist for the Head of Internal Auditing Only

1. What are your relationships with the corporate controller, the audit committee of board of directors, and the external auditors?
2. Is the audit function used as a training ground for future controllers? Do travel requirements pose any difficulty in attracting the right kinds of people?
3. What is the audit procedure used: announced versus unannounced visits, scope (operational, management audit), action taken as a result of audit, special problems?

Additional Checklist for the Executive Working Most Closely with the Company's Financial Control System Only

1. Is an MBO system used? If so, how is it tied to the budget in both planning and performance evaluation? Is bonus based on profitability? If so, is a formula used?
2. Could you describe major components of the company's financial control system? Which of these are *formalized?* Are corporate planning models used?
3. Business planning and budgeting: process. Top down, bottom up? Formal presentations? Budget revisions permitted?
4. Capital expenditures: corporate hurdle rates tailored to business? Harvest and/or divest versus invest and/or grow, and so on? Approval procedure being tightened? Why?
5. Type of data in monthly reports: asset intensity, ROI (adjusted for inflation, replacement cost?), nonaccounting data (competitors' actions, commodity price movements, industry capacity utilization, impact of regulatory developments, discretionary expenditures, that is, advertising, R&D, and so on)?
6. Monthly reports: who explains causes of variance, action being taken? How are the reports used? What is the typical corporate response to large negative variances?

Checklist for the Initial Orientation Interview Only

1. Background and responsibilities of other interviewees.
2. Company history: acquisitions versus internal growth, corporate culture, management's operating and control philosophy.

3. The business: product markets, dominant competitive issues, key success factors, information needs.
4. The company's organization: structure, staffing, development.
5. The control system: budgets (frequency, process, action if variance, budget revisions during year), monthly reporting, other reports to operating managers, capital expenditures.
6. Role and scope of controllership function.
7. The controller's department: organization, staffing, evaluation, training, development, job rotation, line-staff transfers.
8. Divisional controllers: percentage MBA, percentage CPA, line-staff rotations. Does solid versus dotted line matter? Abilities versus tactics versus skills of effective division controllers? Formal evaluation forms? Does company have some division controllers that are much more effective than others? Who?
9. Balance between finance and operations in company (divisions), division-to-division variation, bringing new divisions up to speed, understanding about corporate financial control during acquisition negotiations.
10. Major issues, problems currently facing company. Future challenges.

Checklist for Personnel Executive Most Familiar with the Company's Controllers Only

1. What is effective controllership? Can a company do anything to *develop* effective controllers? What is being done by your company?
2. Hiring and placement of new recruits: CPA, MBA, non-MBA, other graduate, bachelors (accounting, nonaccounting), experienced, other.
3. Bringing above categories on board. Assimilation problems.
4. Training programs for above categories.
5. Planned developmental activities.
6. Career paths (actual versus preferences) for above categories: within finance and control, across other areas, corporate and divisional transfers? Done on a planned basis?
7. Performance evaluation done on a formal basis? How? Where filed? When destroyed?
8. Statistics on division controllers in the company: total, MBA, other graduate, bachelors in accounting, bachelors in nonaccounting, breakdown by previous position held (promoted from within division, was in division when acquired, transferred from sister division, transferred from corporate headquarters, hired from outside), age, experience (in company, total).
9. Controllership personnel in the company as a percentage of total company employment: exempt versus nonexempt at corporate headquarters and at divisional level *(current and over last five years)*.
10. Detailed breakdown of above by functional area, for example, general accounting, cost accounting, EDP, audit, and so on.
11. *Cost* of controllership activity: current and *trend over last five years,* as a percentage of sales, as a percentage of operating expenses.

Bibliography

Aldrich, Howard E., *Organizations and Environments.* Englewood Cliffs, N.J.: Prentice-Hall, 1979.

Allen, L. A., "Improving Line and Staff Relationships." Studies in Personnel Policy No. 153. New York: National Industrial Conference Board, 1956.

Allen, Stephen A. "Organizational Choices and General Management Influence Networks in Divisionalized Companies," *Academy of Management Journal,* 21, no. 3 (September 1978), 341-56.

Anthony, Robert, John Darden, and Richard F. Vancil, *Management Control Systems.* Homewood, Ill.: Irwin, 1972.

Argyris, Chris, *Executive Leadership.* New York: Harper & Row, 1953.

_____, "Personality and Organization Theory Revisited," *Administrative Science Quarterly,* (June 1973), 141-67.

_____, and Donald A. Schon, *Theory in Practice: Increasing Professional Effectiveness.* San Francisco: Jossey-Bass, 1974.

Belasco, James A., and Joseph V. Alutto, "Line-Staff Conflicts: Some Empirical Insights," *Academy of Management Journal,* 12, no. 3 (December 1969), 469-77.

Berg, Norman, "Corporate Role in Diversified Companies." Working Paper, Boston, Mass.: Harvard Business School, 1971.

Blake, Robert R., and Jane S. Mouton, *The Managerial Grid.* Houston: Gulf, 1964.

Blalock, H. M., *Causal Inference in Nonexperimental Research.* New York: W. W. Norton, 1964.

Bowen, D. D., *An Evaluation of Motivational Similarity in Work Groups.* Unpublished Doctoral Dissertation. New Haven, Conn.: Yale University, 1971.

Bower, Joseph L., *Managing the Resource Allocation Process.* Homewood, Ill.: Irwin, 1970.

Bradshaw, T. F., *Developing Men for Controllership.* Cambridge, Mass.: Harvard Univ. Press, 1950.

_____, and C. C. Hull, *Controllership in Modern Management.* Homewood, Ill.: Irwin, 1950.

Brown, Wilfred, *Exploration in Management.* London: Heinemann, 1960.

Business Week, "The Controller: Inflation Gives Him More Clout with Management," August 15, 1977, pp. 84-95.

Campbell, D. T., and D. W. Fiske, "Convergent and Discriminant Validation by the Multitrait-Multimethod Matrix," *Psychological Bulletin,* 56, 1959, 81-105.

Child, John, "Organizational Structure, Environment, and Performance: The Role of Strategic Choice," *Sociology,* 1972, 1-22.

Colins, Orvis, and David G. More, *The Organization Makers.* New York: Appleton-Century-Crofts, 1970.

Crozier, M., *The Bureaucratic Phenomenon.* Chicago: Univer. of Chicago Press, 1964.

Cyert, Richard M., and James March, *A Behavioral Theory of the Firm.* Englewood Cliffs, N.J.: Prentice-Hall, 1963.

Dalton, Melville, *Men Who Manage.* New York: John Wiley, 1959.

Davis, S. M., and Paul R. Lawrence, *Matrix.* Reading, Mass.: Addison-Wesley, 1977.

Dearden, John, *Cost Accounting and Financial Control Systems.* Reading, Mass.: Addison-Wesley, 1973.

Decoster, D. T., and J. G. Rhode, "The Accountant's Stereotype: Real and Imagined, Deserved or Unwarranted," *The Accounting Review,* 46, 1971, 651-62.

Fiedler, F. E., *A Theory of Leadership Effectiveness.* New York: McGraw-Hill, 1967.

Filley, A. C., R. J. House, and S. Kerr, *Managerial Process and Organizational Behavior.* Glenview, Ill.: Scott Foresman, 1976.

Fisch, Gerald G., "Line-Staff Is Obsolete," *Harvard Business Review,* (September-October 1961).

Foulkes, F. K., "The Expanding Role of the Personnel Function," *Harvard Business Review* (March-April 1975), 71-84.

French, Wendell, and Dale A. Henning, "The Authority-Influence Role of the Functional Specialist in Management," *Academy of Management Journal,* 9 (September 1966), 187-203.

Galbraith, Jay, *Designing Complex Organizations.* Reading, Mass.: Addison-Wesley, 1973.

Georgopoulos, Basil S., and Arnold S. Tannenbaum, "The Study of Organizational Effectiveness," *American Sociological Review,* 22, 1957, 534-40.

Gerstner, Louis V., Jr., and M. Helen Anderson, "The Chief Financial Officer as Activist," *Harvard Business Review,* (September-October 1976).

Glaser, B. G., and A. L. Strauss, *The Discovery of Grounded Theory: Strategies for Qualitative Research.* Chicago: Aldine, 1967.

Grimstad, Clayton R., "A Critique," in *The Use of Accounting in Decision Making,* ed. Thomas J. Burns, pp. 163-73. Columbus: Ohio State Univ. Press, 1967.

Hage, J., and M. Aiken, "Relationship of Centralization to Other Structural Properties," *Administrative Science Quarterly,* 12, 1967, 72-92.

Hall, D. T., and R. Mansfield, "Organization and Individual Response to External Stress," *Administrative Science Quarterly,* 1971, 533-47.

Hall, R. H., *Organizations: Structure and Process.* Englewood Cliffs, N.J.: Prentice-Hall, 1972.

Harkins, Edward P., "Organizing and Managing the Corporate Financial Function." Business Policy Study No. 129. New York: National Industrial Conference Board, 1969.

_____, **and G. C. Thompson,** "Problems and Solutions," *The Conference Board Record* (September 1965), 11-16.

Harrell, T. W., *Managers' Performance and Personality.* Cincinnati, Ohio: South-Western, 1961.

Hassler, R. H., and Neil E. Harlan, *Cases in Controllership.* Englewood Cliffs, N.J.: Prentice-Hall, 1958.

Heckert, J. B., *Controllership—The Work of the Accounting Executive.* New York: Ronald Press, 1952.

_____, **and J. D. Willson,** *Business Budgeting and Control.* New York: Ronald Press, 1967.

Helfert, E. A., E. G. May, and M. P. McNair, *Controllership in Department Stores.* Boston: Division of Research, Harvard Business School, 1965.

Henning, D. A., and R. L. Moseley, "Authority Role of a Functional Manager: The Controller," *Administrative Science Quarterly,* 15 (December 1970), 482-89.

Herman, C. F., "Crisis and Organizational Viability," *Administrative Science Quarterly,* 8 (June 1963), 61-82.

Hopper, Trevor, *Role Conflicts of Management Accountants in the Context of their Structural Relationship to Production.* Master of Philosophy Thesis. Birmingham, England: University of Aston, 1978.

Horngren, Charles T., *Cost Accounting: A Managerial Emphasis.* Englewood Cliffs, N.J.: Prentice-Hall, 1967.

Jackson, J. H., *The Comptroller: His Functions and Organization.* Cambridge, Mass.: Harvard Univ. Press, 1949.

Jannell, Paul A., and Raymond R. Kinnunen, "Portrait of the Division Controller," *Management Accounting,* (June 1980), 15-19.

Jenkins, W. O., "A Review of Leadership Studies with Particular Reference to Military Problems," *Psychological Bulletin,* 44, 1947, 54-79.

Kanter, Rosabeth Moss, "Power Failure in Management Circuits," *Harvard Business Review,* 59, (July-August 1979), 65-75.

Katz, Daniel, and Robert L. Kahn, *The Social Psychology of Organizations* (2nd ed.). New York: John Wiley, 1978.

Koontz, Harold, and Cyril O'Donnell, *Principles of Management.* New York: McGraw-Hill, 1978.

Kotter, J. P., "Power, Dependence, and Effective Management," *Harvard Business Review* (July-August 1977), 125-36.

Lawler, Edward E., III, "Control Systems in Organizations," in *Handbook of Industrial and Organizational Psychology,* ed. Marvin D. Dunnette. Chicago: Rand McNally, 1976.

_____, and J. G. Rhode, *Information and Control in Organizations.* Santa Monica, Calif.: Goodyear, 1976.

Lawrence, Paul R., "The Harvard Organization and Environment Research Program." Working Paper. Boston, Mass.: Harvard Business School, 1980.

_____, and Jay W. Lorsch, *Organization and Environment: Managing Differentiation and Integration.* Boston: Division of Research, Harvard Business School, 1967.

Litterer, Joseph A., *The Analysis of Organizations.* New York: John Wiley, 1973.

Livingstone, J. Leslie, and Vijay Sathe, "A New View of the Controller's Organization," *Proceedings of the Conference on Topical Research in Accounting.* New York: New York University Press, 1976.

Logan, H. H., "Line and Staff: An Obsolete Concept?" *Personnel* (January-February 1966), 26-33.

Lorsch, J. W., and Stephen A. Allen, III, *Managing Diversity and Interdependence: An Organizational Study of Multi-Divisional Firms.* Boston: Division of Research, Harvard Business School, 1973.

Lynch, B. P., "An Empirical Assessment of Perrow's Technology Construct," *Administrative Science Quarterly,* 19, 1974, 338-56.

MacDonald, J. H., *Controllership: Its Functions and Technique.* New York: Controllers Institute of America, 1940.

March, J. G., and H. A. Simon, *Organizations.* New York: John Wiley, 1958.

McClelland, D. C., *The Achieving Society.* New York: Van Nostrand, 1961.

McDonough, J. J., "The Accountant: Data Collection and Social Exchange," *Accounting Review,* 46 (May-June 1971), 676-85.

McGregor, Douglas, *The Human Side of Enterprise.* New York: McGraw-Hill, 1960.

McKenna, E. F., *Management Style of Chief Accountant.* Farnborough, England: Teakfield, 1979.

Minard, L., and B. McGlyn, "The U.S.'s Newest Glamour Job," *Forbes,* September 1, 1977, 32-36.

Mintzberg, H., *The Structuring of Organizations: A Research Emphasis.* Englewood Cliffs, N.J.: Prentice-Hall, 1979.

Moseley, R., "The Controller—A Mythical Executive," *Management Accounting,* 46 (March 1972), 676-85.

Mott, Paul E., *The Characteristics of Effective Organizations.* New York: Harper & Row, 1972.

Mruk, E. S., and J. A. Giardina, "Compensating Financial Management," *Financial Executive* (September 1977), 50-54.

Nunnally, Jum C., *Psychometric Theory.* New York: McGraw-Hill, 1968.

Pennings, Johannes M., "Organizational Effectiveness: A Behavioral View," Book Review in *Administrative Science Quarterly,* 22 (1977), 538-40.

Perrow, Charles, "A Framework for the Comparative Analysis of Organizations," *American Sociological Review,* 32 (1967), 194-208.

Pettigrew, A., "Information Control as a Power Resource," *Sociology,* 6 (1972), 187-204.

Pointdexter, J., "The New Controllers: More than Numbers," *Dun's Review,* 94 (October 1969), 37-41.

Porter, L. W., and E. E. Lawler, *Managerial Attitudes and Performance* (Homewood, Ill.: Irwin-Dorsey), 1968.

Robbins, S. M., and R. B. Stobaugh, "Growth of the Financial Function," *Financial Executive* (June 1973), 12-19.

Rumelt, R. P., *Strategy, Structure, and Economic Performance.* Boston: Division of Research, Harvard Business School, 1974.

Sherwin, Douglas, "The Meaning of Control," *Modern Industry* (January 1956).

Silverman, G. W., "Financial Training Rises to the Top," *Financial Executive* (November 1975), 32-37.

Sathe, Vijay, *Controllership in Divisionalized Firms: Structure, Evaluation, and Development.* New York: AMACOM, 1978a.

_____, "Who Should Control Division Controllers?" *Harvard Business Review* (September-October 1978b).

Simon, Herbert A., *Administrative Behavior.* New York: Free Press, 1945.

_____, H. Guetzkow, G. Kozmetsky, and G. Tyndall, *Centralization vs. Decentralization in Organizing the Controller's Department.* New York: Controllership Foundation, 1954.

Sorter, G. H., and S. W. Becker, "Corporate Personality as Reflected in Accounting Decisions: Some Preliminary Findings," *Journal of Accounting Research,* 2 (1964), 183-96.

Steers, Richard M., "Problems in Measurement of Organizational Effectiveness," *Administrative Science Quarterly,* 20 (1975), 546-58.

Stoddard, F. Don, "The Accountant's Role in Management," *Management Accounting,* (July 1978), 42-45.

Stoughton, Warner V., "Bringing Up Management Accountants," *Management Accounting,* (June 1978). 55-59.

Strauss, George, "Tactics of Lateral Relationship: The Purchasing Agent," *Administrative Science Quarterly,* (1962), 161-86.

Susman, Gerald I., and Roger D. Evered, 1978, "An Assessment of the Scientific Merits of Action Research," *Administrative Science Quarterly,* 23 (1978), 582-603.

Thompson, James D. *Organizations in Action.* New York: McGraw-Hill, 1967.

Tuckey, John W., *Exploratory Data Analysis.* Reading, Mass.: Addison-Wesley, 1977.

Urwick, Lyndall F., "The Meaning of Control," *Michigan Business Review,* 12 (November 1960), 9-13.

Vroom, V. H., *Work and Motivation.* New York: John Wiley, 1964.

Williamson, Oliver E., *Markets and Hierarchies: Analysis and Antitrust Implications.* New York: Free Press, 1975.

Woodward, Joan, *Industrial Organization: Theory and Practice.* London: Oxford University Press, 1965.

Wrigley, Leonard, "Divisional Autonomy and Diversification." Unpublished Doctoral Dissertation. Boston, Mass.: Harvard Business School, 1970.

Index

Accounting, 14, 151
  replacement cost, 2
  surprises, 28, 30, 32, 82
Acquisitions, 10
Advanced Management Program
  (Harvard), 74
Advertising, 9
Agencies, regulatory, 1, 2, 152, 153
  reports to, and importance of
    controller independence, 17,
    81-82
Aiken, M., 60n
Allen, Stephen, A., 52n, 54, 65n, 91n,
  104n, 163, 165
Alutto, Joseph V., 12n
Anderson, M. Helen, 11n
Argyris, Chris, 22n, 82n, 121
Asset management, 1, 54, 66, 69-70.
  See also Financial management
Audit committee, 149
Auditing
  internal, and independence of
    controller, 18-19, 84
  rules and reporting requirements, 2,
    152, 153
Authority, staff (functional), 14-15

Bankruptcy, near, history of, 28, 31-33,
  42-44

Bargaining, as tactic, 15
Belasco, James A., 12n
Berg, Norman, 53, 68n
Blake, Robert R., 124n
Blalock, H. M., 60n
Bookkeeping, 12
  separation of, from service functions,
    116
Bowen, D. D., 72n
Bower, Joseph L., 69n
Bradshaw, T. F., 11n, 18n, 122n
Brown, Wilfred, 14n, 15n
Budgeting, controller role in, 9, 65
Business. *See also* Company(ies)
  illegal activities in, 1-2, 17-18, 19,
    25-26, 29, 129
  problems of. *See specific topic, e.g.,*
    Inflation; Recession
  unit, defined, 51
Business school graduates, 11, 144
Business Week, 10-11

Campbell, D. T., 60n
Capital
  management. *See* Financial
    management
  shortages, 1, 53, 69
Career paths, 147-48
Centralization, 91

Change. *See* Company(ies), rate of change in
Child, John, 54, 120n
Command, chains of, 14-15, 22, 49-51, 151, 152
Company(ies)
 acquisition (conglomerates), 68
 centralization and decentralization in, 91
 divisions of, corporate role in, 91-97
  feasibility of, 95-96
  and perception of risked posed by division, 94-95
 large, diversification strategies of, 53, 65
 matrix, 15
 multidivision, and intracompany transfers, 10, 53, 65
 operating interdependence in, 52, 53, 65-68, 79, 99
 performance of, controller involvement and, 21-22
  and controller independence, 25-27
  correlated with degrees of risk taking and control, 27-44, 127
  financial, 22-23
  management creativity and, 23-25
 rate of change in, 52, 53, 65, 66, 79, 88, 99, 101
 in study, profile of, 3, 4, 62-63. *See also* Study
Compensation practices, 12
Competitive advantage, effectiveness and, 124
Computers, 11
Conflict resolution, 85-86, 89, 90
Confrontation, 85-86, 89, 90
Conglomerates, 68
Conservatism. *See* Risk taking
Contingency theory of organization, 119-20
Continuing education and training, 145-46
Control, 27-29, 38-39, 53, 54, 151. *See also* Financial management
 balance of, 127
 consequences of high
  with high risk taking, 34, 35, 36-38
  with low risk taking, 31-34, 42-44
 consequences of low
  with high risk taking, 31, 41-42
  with low risk taking, 29-31, 40-41

Control (*cont.*)
 defined, 69n
 degree of
  defined, 29
  and degree of controller involvement, 66, 69-70, 79, 100
 expense, 54
 and management's expectations, 81-82
 reactive and anticipatory, 18-19, 36, 131, 137, 154
Controller, corporate, 2. *See also* Controller, generally
 ability and motivation of, 84-85
 characteristics of, 83-86, 148-50
 defined, 9
 effects of contextual factors on involvement of, 64-77
  and degree of operating interdependence, 65-68, 79
  and financial analysis and control, 66, 69-70, 79
  and management's expectations, 67, 75-83
  and management's financial ability, 67, 70-75, 79, 125-26
  and management's financial orientation, 67, 72-75, 79
  and rate of change in business environment, 65, 66, 79
 in high risk taking, high control companies, 34, 35
 position in chain of command, 49-50
 relationships with division controllers, 26-27, 105-11, 138
  degree of formal authority over, 105, 106, 108
  and emphasis on personnel development, 107, 109-11
  and emphasis on service role, 106, 108-109, 138
  and expectations regarding involvement, 106, 108
 responsibilities of, 19, 49-50. *See also* role of
  time allocation to, 83-84
 role of, 148-50
 style of, 85-86
Controller, division, 2. *See also* Controller, generally
 career paths of, 147-48
 continuing education and training for, 145-46

Controller division (*cont.*)
  defined, 9
  development of strong characteristics
      in, 140-48
  effects of contextual factors on
      involvement of, 87-97, 98-111
  and corporate controller's
      emphasis on personnel
      development, 107, 109-11
  and corporate controller's
      emphasis on service role, 106,
      108-109, 138
  and corporate controller's
      expectations, 106, 108
  and corporate controller's formal
      authority, 105, 106, 108
  and degree of operating
      interdependence, 99, 101
  and financial analysis and control,
      100, 101
  and management's emphasis on
      controllership-line transfers,
      102, 104-105
  and management's expectations,
      88, 89, 90, 101, 104
  and management's financial
      orientation, 102, 103-104,
      125-26
  and management's operating style,
      102, 104
  and rate of change in business
      environment, 88, 89, 99, 101
  evaluating and weeding, 146-47
  in high risk taking, high control
      companies, 34, 35
  placement and progression of, 144
  position in chain of command, 50,
      51
  recruitment and selection of, 144
  relationships with corporate
      controllers, 26-27, 105-11, 138
  responsibilities of, 19, 50, 51, 128-
      29. *See also* role of
  time allocation to, 89, 90
  role of, 129-39
      changing, 137-39
      criteria for determining, 134-37
      types of, 130-34
  style of, 89, 90
Controller, generally. *See also*
      Controller, corporate;
      Controller, division; Controller,
      plant
  and chain of command, 49-51

Controller, generally (*cont.*)
  contextual factors, effects of, and
      scope and method of study,
      45-49, 64-65. *See also* Study
  defined, 8
  history of, 6-7, 10-16
  image of, stereotypical, 13, 147-48
  independence of
      effect of, on company
          performance, 25-27
      importance of, 17-20
  involvement in decision making. *See
      also* Decision making
      correlated with risk taking,
          control, and company
          performance, 27-44
      defined, 9-10
      importance of, and other studies,
          10-16, 115-16. *See also* Study
  power and influence of, 16-17
  and reactive and anticipatory
      control, 18-19, 36, 131, 137,
      154
  responsibilities of, 1-2, 9, 18-19, 49-
      51
      compared with treasurer, 7-8
      secondary, 9-10
Controllers Institute of America, 7
Controller, plant, 9. *See also* Controller,
      generally
  position in chain of command, 51
  responsibilities of, 19, 51
Cost accounting, replacement, 2
Credibility, 36
Credit, 9
Crozier, M., 15n
Cyert, Richard M., 22n

Dalton, Melville, 14n
Data collection and analysis in study,
      58-61. *See also* Study
Davis, S. M., 15n, 135n, 145, 146
Decentralization, 91
Decision making, 1
  company performance and controller
      involvement in, 9-10, 17, 21-22
  correlated with risk taking and
      control, 27-44, 127
  effect of controller independence
      on, 25-27
  financial performance, 22-23
  management creativity and, 23-25
  conflicts in. *See* Conflict resolution

Decision making (*cont.*)
  formal authority and, 14-15, 22
  independence vs. involvement in, 17-20
  influence vs. involvement in, 16-17
  informal authority and, 15-16
De Coster, D. T., 13n
Directors, liability of, 19
Discipline, functional authority and, 14-15
Distribution, 9
Diversification strategies, 53, 65
Division, defined, 51. *See also*
      Company(ies); Controller, division
Dun's Review, 11

Education and training, continuing, 145-46
Effectiveness, examining staff and organizational, 120-25
Engineering, 151
Entrepreneurship, 31
Environment, corporate. *See* Company(ies)
Equity, stockholders', 1
Ethical questions, 120-21
Evered, Roger D., 121n
Executives. *See* Management
Expectations. *See* Management, expectations of
Expense control, 54

Filley, A. C., 15n
Financial ability of management, defined, 72. *See also* Management
Financial analysis, 1, 9, 11, 66, 69-70, 79, 100, 101. *See also* Financial management
Financial Executives Institute, 7
Financial control, defined, 69n. *See also* Control
Financial management, 1. *See also* Control
  and analysis and control, importance of, 66, 69-70, 79, 100, 101
  and border with operations, 11
  and controllership and treasurership functions compared, 7-8
  criticality of, 53-54

Financial management (*cont.*)
  and degree of controller involvement, effects of, 22-23
  correlated with risk taking and control, 27-44, 127
  and integrity of reporting and internal control, 81-82
  orientation of management to, 53, 54, 67, 72-75, 79, 102, 103-104
  defined, 72
Fisch, Gerald G., 15n
Fiske, D. W., 60n
Forbes "30th Annual Report on American Industry," 55
Foreign Corrupt Practices Act of 1977, 1-2, 18, 81, 129
Fraud, 29, 32. *See also* Business, illegal activities in
French, Wendell, 15n
Functional authority, 14-15

Gabarro, John J., 146
Galbraith, Jay, 52n
General managers, responsibilities of, 19. *See also* Management
Georgopoulous, Basil S., 124n
Gerstner, Louis V., Jr., 11n
Giardina, J. A., 12n
Glaser, B. G., 46n, 61
Governmental regulations. *See* Agencies, regulatory
Guetzkow, H., 12n, 91n, 116n

Hage, J., 60n
Hall, D. T., 82n, 83n
Hall, R. H., 117n
Harkins, Edward P., 7-8, 11n, 69n
Harlan, Neil E., 13n
Harrell, T. W., 13n
Harvard Business Review, 11
Harvard University, 74
Hassler, R. H., 13n
Heckert, J. B., 6, 65n
Helfert, E. A., 12
Henning, Dale A., 15n
Herman, C. F., 22n, 82n
Hopper, Trevor, 12, 54n, 116
Horngren, Charles T., 65n
House, R. J., 15n
Hull, C. C., 18n, 122n

Illegal payments, 1
Inflation, 1, 11
  and criticality of financial
    management, 53-54, 69
Internal cash generation, 11
Interviews. *See* Study
Inventory, 9
Investments, 9-10

Jackson, J. H., 11n, 122n
Jannell, Paul A., 140n, 144n
Jenkins, W. O., 117n

Kahn, Robert L., 54n, 75n, 90n, 108n,
    116n, 117n, 118, 119n
Kanter, Rosabeth Moss, 16, 135n
Katz, Daniel, 54n, 75n, 90n, 108n,
    116n, 117n, 118, 119n
Kerr, S., 15n
Kickbacks, 1
Kinnunen, Raymond R., 140n, 144n
Kolodny, Harvey, 146
Koontz, Harold, 13n, 14n
Kotter, John P., 16, 135n, 146
Kozmetsky, G., 12n, 91n, 116n

Law, as specialist work, 14, 151
Lawler, Edward E., 13n, 15, 69n, 136n
Lawrence, Paul R., 15n, 52n, 85n, 86n,
    117n, 124n, 125, 135n, 145,
    146, 167
Liability, personal, 19, 152-53
Line and staff positions
  definitions of, 151-52
  literature on, 13-16
  and staff-line conflicts, 14
Litterer, Joseph A., 14n
Logan, H. H., 15n
Lorsch, J. W., 52n, 54, 65n, 85n, 86n,
    91n, 104n, 117n, 124n, 125,
    145n, 163, 167
Lynch, B. P., 61n

McClelland, D. C., 117n
McGregor, Douglas, 16, 18n, 130n,
    135n
McKenna, E. F., 15
McNair, M. P., 12n
Management, 9. *See also* Command,
    chains of
  corporate
    availability of, to division, 95-96

Management (*cont.*)
  and changes in role of division
    controller, 138-39
  familiarity of, with division's
    business, 94-95
  creativity, stifling of, 23-25, 28, 34,
    44, 131-34, 136
  dependence of, on controllers, 1, 152
  and demand for information, 52,
    53
  division, 151
    corporate controllers and, 26-27
    performance of, 95
    power of, 95
  egotistical, 29, 31, 126
  expectations of, 53, 54
    and controller independence, 81-
    83
    and controller involvement, 67,
    75-81, 88, 89, 90, 100, 102,
    104
  financial ability of, 67, 70-75, 79,
    100, 102, 103, 125-26
    defined, 72
    and inbreeding, 126-27
  financial orientation of, 53, 54, 67,
    72-75, 79, 100, 102, 103-104
    defined, 72
  general, responsibilities of, 19
  inbreeding of, 126-27
  independence from, 1, 17-20
    effect of, on company
    performance, 25-27
    and management's expectations,
    81-83
  interpersonal relationships with, 13,
    24
  liability of, 19, 152-53
  line and staff defined, and literature
    on, 13-16
  operating philosophy of, 53, 54, 100,
    102, 104-105
  personnel, 12, 14, 15
  risk-averse. *See* Risk taking
  staff role in, 151-54
  and substitution effect, 125-26
Mansfield, R., 82n, 83n
March, James, 22n, 82n
Matrix organizations, 15
May, E. G., 12n
MBAs, 11, 144

Methodology of study, 54-63. *See also*
Study
Moseley, R. L., 8n, 15n
Mott, Paul E., 124n
Mouton, Jane S., 124n
Mruk, E. S., 12n

National Industrial Conference Board,
11
Nunnally, J. C., 60n

O'Donnell, Cyril, 13n, 14n
Operating roles, 151-52
Operations, 11, 14. *See also* Command,
chains of; Management
Organizational setting of study, 49-51.
See also Command, chains of;
Study
Organization theory, 117-25
contingency, 119-20
descriptive, 117-20
prescriptive, 120-25
role theory and, 117-19
and staff and organizational
effectiveness, 122-25

Pennings, Johannes M., 124n
Personal liability, 19, 152-53
Personnel development
corporate controller's emphasis on,
and division controller
involvement, 107, 109-11
of strong division controllers, 140-48
Personnel managers, 12, 14, 15, 151
Persuasion, 15-16
Pettigrew, A., 15n
Planning, annual, controller role in, 9
Poindexter, J., 11n
Pricing, 9
of intracompany sales, 53, 65
Production, as line position, 151
Product(s)
distribution, 9
inventory, 9
liability claims, 3
new, 9
operations work and, 14
pricing, 9
promotion, 9
Profit and loss reporting, 2
Profitability. *See* Company(ies),
performance of
Promotion, product, 9

Public pressure, 81-82
Public relations, 14, 151
Purchasing, 151

Quality assurance, 151
Questionnaires. *See* Study

Recession, 1, 11
Replacement cost accounting, 2
Reporting requirements, 2
controller independence and, 17-20
Research, as specialist work, 14, 151
Rhode, J. G., 13n, 15, 69n
Risk taking, 27-29, 38-39
balance of, 127
consequences of high
with high control, 34, 35, 36-38
with low control, 31, 41-42
consequences of low
with high control, 31-34, 42-44
with low control, 29-31, 40-41
degree of, defined, 28, 29
Role theory
expectations and, 54
implications of study for, 116, 117-
19
Rumelt, R. P., 53, 65n, 68

Sales, 151
Sathe, Vijay, 55n, 139n, 146
Schon, Donald A., 121n
Securities and Exchange Commission,
122, 152
Service functions, 12, 16
corporate controller's emphasis on,
and division controller's
involvement, 106, 108-
109
separation of, from bookkeeping
functions, 116
Sherwin, Douglas, 69n
Silverman, G. W., 72n
Simon, Herbert A., 12, 82n, 91n, 116n,
120
Specialists, work of, 14
Staff, generally, 2-3
authority, 14-15
effectiveness of, examining, 122-24
independence, 20
and line positions, literature on, 13-
16
role of, in management, 151-54
and staff-line conflicts, 14

Status, 12
Steers, Richard M., 124n
Stewardship, 13
Stockholders' equity, 1
Stoddard, F. Don, 140n
Stoughton, Warner V., 140n
Strauss, A. L., 46n, 61
Strauss, George, 16
Stress, environmental, 82-83
Study
    conceptual framework of, 52-54,
        113, 115
    focus of, 8, 51-52
    implications of, practical, 128-54
        and development of strong
            division controllers, 140-48
        and roles of corporate controllers,
            148-50
        and roles of division controllers,
            129-39
        and staff roles in management,
            generally, 151-54
    implications of, for research and
        theory, 115-27
        and contingency theory of
            organization, 119-20
        and organizational effectiveness,
            124-25
        and prescriptive organization
            theory, 120-25
        and research on controller
            involvement, 115-16
        and role theory, 117-19
        and staff effectiveness, 122-24
        and unanswered questions, 125-27

Study (*cont.*)
    methods and organization of, 3-4,
        10, 47-48, 54-63, 155-76
    data collection and analysis, 58-
        61
    presentation and discussion of
        results, 61-63
    and variables measured via
        interviews, 170-76
    and variables measured via
        published documents, 158-59
    and variables measured via
        questionnaires, 159-69
    nomenclature for, 155-57
    and other studies, 10-16, 115-16
    scope and limitations of, 2-3, 9, 45-
        46, 49-51
Susman, Gerald I., 121n

Tannenbaum, Arnold S., 124n
Thompson, G. C., 69n
Thompson, James D., 52n, 117n
Title, 12
Training and continuing education, 145-
    46
Treasurership, compared with
    controllership, 7-8, 68
Trust, importance of, 24, 36
Tuckey, John W., 59n
Tyndall, G., 12n, 91n, 116n

Variables measured in study. *See* Study

Ware, James P., 146
Willson, J. D., 6, 65n
Wrigley, Leonard, 53, 65n